Young Man, You Forgot Your Overcoat

or

Around the World in Fifty Years

Colm Madden

For Shelley and Erika.

"There are no foreign lands. It is the traveler only who is
foreign."
–Robert Louis Stevenson

Contents

Chapter One

Pakistan, and Memories of Home

"Young man! Young man!" I heard a distant voice calling out faintly from behind me as I hurried through the crowded corridors of London's Heathrow Airport, towards the departure gate, where boarding of the Pakistan International Airlines flight bound for Karachi, Pakistan, was already underway. The voice was female and, to my ears at least, seemed of a somewhat advanced age. I was uncertain this call was directed at me until the lady quickly followed up with the comment, "Young man, young man, you forgot your overcoat."

I looked back in the direction from where the voice had come and sure enough, there she was, a little old lady in possession of my tattered Irish tweed overcoat, making a valiant effort to catch up with me and return it. She was small and not particularly stylishly dressed; in fact, she could have been described as just a little frumpy. Her brown threadbare coat that reached to her ankles and the battered felt hat she wore, noticably stood out among the 'suited and booted' airline travellers of the nineteen sixties, who crowded the corridors as they made their way to the variety of departures gates and flights destined for all corners of the world. She might very well not have been that old, but when you're aged twenty-three, anyone over fifty who doesn't look like a movie star or fashion model, or make some attempt to camouflage the march of time, might be viewed as having already lived the majority of their life, with one foot in this world and one in the next.

I had not forgotten the coat but had deliberately left it on the seat in the crowded departure lounge of the international terminal. Despite my best efforts to lose it, it was now back in my possession, turning up like a bad penny, albeit much less valuable and more cumbersome. Out of consideration for the dear lady's efforts and my own sense of embarrassment in the midst of a curious crowd, I was obliged to accept it. Though I smiled my thanks, beneath my appreciative façade lurked a tiny touch of annoyance.

I'm off to live and work in a country where an overcoat is fiction, and I'm burdened with one best consigned to the garbage bin. This will make for a strange image upon my arrival at Karachi airport in temperatures north of twenty degrees centigrade, dressed as if ready for the onslaught of a northern winter.

Coming from Ireland, temperatures in January above single digits centigrade were perceived as warm. It was January 28, 1966, and I, Colm Madden, left the family home in Mount Merrion, County Dublin, Ireland, earlier that morning in weather conditions that only exist there: damp, bone-chilling cold that burrows its way through the warmest clothing and penetrates the very core of one's existence, all under the umbrella of a dark, grey sky. In later years, I would live in much colder climates, but none compare to the misery of a wet, wind-driven, sleet-loaded, Irish winter day. It is uniquely unpleasant.

On the first leg of the journey, from Mount Merrion to Dublin Airport, about twenty miles away in North Co. Dublin, in those days just a small single terminal airport located among the green farmland of North Co. Dublin, the tattered old tweed overcoat had offered some protection from the cold, so for that, I was grateful. If I remained in Ireland, the time was ripe for a new coat.

From Dublin Airport, I would have a short one-and-a-half-hour Aer Lingus flight to London Heathrow Airport and then, that same evening, onwards with Pakistan International Airways to Karachi, Pakistan. Awaiting the flight to Karachi in the warmth of the busy airport with the hustle and bustle of travellers vying for seats or viewing the vast area of duty free shops, was a happy respite from the earlier cold. I eagerly anticipated the hot weather to come. It was the first time I was to live permanently outside the family home, and in those days, before the concept of the 'Global Village' existed, it was the most exotic and far-reaching location no one I knew, or knew of, had been to.

Well, so I thought at the time!

Here I was, fulfilling a kind of fantasy. I was held in awe by my friends who laboured in safe positions with predictably successful futures in and around the Dublin area. And I was worried over by my parents who respected my decision to go, but probably wished I had sought a position with a safe, predictable, and potentially successful future at home in Dublin. But I felt fearless; after all, I was only twenty-three, was quite accomplished in my short career, and had my whole life ahead of me. As with many young men of my age, I was convinced I was invincible and knew without question I was setting out on a grand adventure. Life could not have been sweeter.

Well, almost! I was disappointed that Pauline, my girlfriend of two years, had decided to wait six months before joining me, but that was the only dark cloud on an otherwise bright horizon. Pauline was a few years older than I, an attractive, sophisticated, sexy, stylish blonde who worked as a window dresser for a fashion house in Dublin. Our relationship moved me away from the friends I had grown up with, into a different social circle, to spend time in newly acquainted friend's homes, actually Pauline's friends' homes, restaurants, bars, and night clubs. We would also spend our weekend days and sometimes nights together, in summer at the beach and in winter on walks or drives to the Wicklow hills. We wasted not a minute apart. Our relationship was intense and if our time was a generation later, we might have lived together. However in the nineteen sixties in 'Catholic' Ireland, that was not done outside of marriage, so our intimacy remained clandestine.

I better get a move on, or I'll miss the flight. I hadn't given myself a great deal of time, and the encounter with the lady returning the old overcoat had delayed me further. I arrived at the departure gate just in time and boarded the plane, wearing my new tropical suit and soft leather shoes while reluctantly carrying the old coat. The checked-in suitcase contained six new white tropical shirts, six new cotton boxer shorts, six pairs of new socks, six new handkerchiefs, and a lightweight suit, new clothes for the new tropical adventure.

I had flown on only a few previous occasions, all between Ireland and England and none of the flights lasting more than an hour or so. This was a wholly different experience: sixteen hours to Karachi, with stops in Geneva, Beirut, and Teheran. The sights, smells, and sounds I encountered as I climbed the ramp and entered the PIA Boeing 707 were very new to me. They were the first introduction of my senses to the world I was to become familiar with and eventually connected to in the coming years and beyond. The exotic clothes of the women, their colourful silk saris, and elegant shalwar kamizes, a rainbow of colours, the pyjamas and kurtas of the men, with a smattering of people dressed in suits and dresses, the high level of chatter in languages I didn't understand and had never heard before, and the scents of spices were all strange to me. As a young man from Dublin, Ireland, at that time, in the mid-sixties, a somewhat provincial capital in a somewhat insular country, with little exposure to other cultures, I had never experienced such sights or sounds. They fuelled my excitement and contributed to my conviction that the decision to leave my homeland and the predictable future that it most likely held, was the right one. I had the courage to do this, to jump into the journey with belief in myself, the desire to live life fully, and confidence in my ability to succeed. Was it a kind of arrogance, a blind faith and a youthful naiveté? Whatever it was, I was now onboard this flight to the rest of my life, and there was no turning back.

In those days, long flights such as the one I was embarking upon from London to Karachi were not 'nonstop'; there would be several stops along the way for refuelling and the boarding of additional passengers. So, I sat back and relaxed, my mind conjuring up the future and drifting to the past. What might the Karachi InterContinental Hotel where I was going to work on contract for the next two years be like. What will be the similarities and the differences to the Dublin Hotel in Ballsbridge? I conjured up images of my destination; swaying palm trees, white sandy beaches, azure blue water. How strange would it be, how different from my home? I let my mind wander to Pauline. Would she eventually join me, as we had discussed? I was unsure as she had wavered during conversations. I thought about my parents, about my friends, and about the life I was leaving behind, and I wondered about the life to come. Eventually, I drifted off to sleep.

I awoke with a start as the plane touched down gently on the runway at Geneva Airport, our first stop, where an hour's wait was anticipated and additional passengers would join the flight. Though the plane was almost full, there were a small number of empty seats, including one beside me. I hoped it would remain so, as it provided a little extra stretching room. Unfortunately, it did not. Additional passengers soon began boarding, and one lone male of approximately forty years of age settled himself into the seat beside me. In my comfort zone, small talk was close to anathema; I was comfortable being alone and uncomfortable with idle chatter, so I kept my eyes closed in the hope that there would be no attempt at conversation by my new neighbour. However, it would prove considerably challenging to pretend to be asleep for the next dozen or more hours.

A couple of hours into the flight from Geneva, drinks and dinner were served, so as soon as I opened my eyes, my neighbour jumped at the chance to start a conversation. Introducing himself as Klaus, he asked, "coming from London?" While I made a rather feeble effort to avoid eye contact and pretend I didn't hear him, that failed. He repeated the question.

"No from Dublin, and you?" I was forced to respond.. I hoped my bluntness would dissuade him, It didn't.

"From Munich."

I felt I was being sucked into a conversation I had hoped to avoid.

" I'm going to work at the Karachi InterContinental Hotel and what do you do"? He continued.

"Me too, as laundry manager," I replied.

A strange coincidence, two people meeting on a plane as strangers and there is a commonality of purpose, of destination, and even of work life. Klaus and I now had work on which to establish the basis for a fractured conversation during the remainder of the journey. We would share a flat for a brief time in Karachi, but rarely saw each other and never became friends. Klaus was part of a tightly knit kitchen brigade, and I had my own responsibilities and little contact with kitchen staff.

Following touchdown at Karachi Airport, the subsequent drive to the hotel, my first experience outside Europe, was startling. The hordes of people that thronged the roads, mostly of men dressed in kurta pyjamas, interspersed with a smattering of women, some covered from head to toe in black burkas, overwhelmed my senses. The camel carts that plodded along seemed from a bygone era. They slowed the vehicular traffic of highly painted and decorated trucks, black and yellow motor rickshaws, and the multitude of cycle rickshaws weaving their way through the traffic of some new, but mostly ancient cars that chaotically ignored all road etiquette, or any traffic rules that might have existed. Contributing to the chaos were blaring horns and angry shouts. The buildings, mostly blocks of flats, and though painted in a variety of pastel colours, they were moulding, like wilting summer flowers in the autumn. The smells I encountered were pungent and unpleasant, and the dusty beige open and unloved grassless spaces depressed me. And all this under a cloudless sky and a relentless burning sun that scorched the earth. Where was the greenery? There was little in this city in the desert. It was a startling change of environment and an immediate and intense culture shock.

More than half a century earlier, my paternal grandfather along with his family landed in the same city, so maybe there was an unseen force that drew me to this place.

My grandfather, Dennis Madden, was a sergeant with the Connaught Rangers Regiment of the British Army during the time of the Raj. He arrived in Karachi, probably in 1908, along with his wife Annie, his eldest son Christy, and Patrick my father. The city would have been a very different place then, although the dust, the camel carts and the blazing sun would have mirrored today.

When Dennis Madden was initially identified for a posting in India, he and his family first travelled to a tour of duty in Malta for two years, and subsequently by steamship through the Suez Canal to Karachi. My father was just a little more than two years old at the time, and several of his younger brothers were born in India, as the family lived there for about eight years.

When I was a child, my father would return home from work in the evening and would delight my siblings and I with stories of his life as a boy in India: the family summer trips by covered wagon up into the hills beyond Peshawar, now in Pakistan, to escape the heat of the plains; how Dodi, their servant, would take him to the bazaar for shopping; how he helped make chapatis for breakfast; and the occasion when he was bitten by a poisonous snake and Dodi cut out a piece from the back of his leg to suck out the poison and save his life.

Regardless of my families earlier connection to this country, it was of course, still foreign to me and I began to question my decision. Was I as brave and adventurous as I thought? But the decision had been made, the die had been cast, and no choice remained. I would battle with determination, through the strangeness, and the homesickness that gripped the muscles of my stomach,.

I was assigned a room at the InterContinental Hotel for a week, and was introduced and integrated into the hotel and my own department. At that time the hotel was about two years old, a retangular building, set in generously proportioned gardens, and adorned with Islamic architectural influences. It had three hundred rooms and several bars, restaurants and banquet facilities and was located about four kilometres from Karachi city centre.

I moved into a furnished flat with Klaus, which was provided by the hotel, and moved out of the flat after a month. It was too large, unfurnished apart from my bedroom, and had an unappealing feel about it, with more space than needed.. My first encounter with lizards was in that flat and one morning I awoke to a rather large one in the bathroom which stared at me and startled me. Later, I was to learn that they were harmless, rather useful, as they ate bugs, mosquitos and other unpleasant insects.

I couldn't cook, had never lived alone before, and was somewhat at a loss as to how to provide for myself, so I moved into a small residential hotel near the InterContinental, a five-minute walk to work. The hotel had ten or twelve rooms that were small and quite flimsily constructed from wood, but it was clean, cheap and had an excellent restaurant. When off duty, I would regularly eat there. When at work, I had my meals in the InterContinental Hotel coffee shop.

During my early weeks in Karachi I felt very alone and lost in an unfamiliar society and I missed the company of Pauline particularly and of my family.

I thought about Pauline, I reminisced on the totality of my youth even before Pauline. My youth in Ireland that was gone forever, for I had now stepped into the world of independent responsibility: my friendship with the girls and guys in that part of my life was over, the platonic friendships and the romantic ones. Like Rosemary and Adrienne. The magnificent Adrienne Kelly was a favourite dance partner. She was arguably the best dancer and prettiest girl among the hundred or more girls who frequented the clubs I went to. She was beautiful, tall and elegant, with long flowing dark blond ringlets and stunning features. She was a magnet for every male in the club; however, she never seemed to be on a date, or have a permanent male companion, always arriving at the clubs with one or two of her female friends.. On several occasions, she would ask me if I would drop her and her girlfriends home after the dance to North Dublin City. I always happily agreed. It also provided the opportunity to ask for a date. However, in spite of our friendship and my most charming requests, she always refused me. Adrienne's dancing friendship with me continued for a time, but still no date, except the occasion we attended a black tie ball in the Gresham Hotel, and no other male companion. Was she 'in the closet'? If so, it was a fact she might have preferred to keep to herself. This was Ireland in the early sixties!

I also thought of Rosemary my very close platonic friend, she was my buddy, and how my father, without cause misjudged us and added a 'crack in the wall' of my relationship with him. On one evening, after seeing me in the local cinema with her, who he knew to be several years older than me, and I didn't return home until four a.m. the following morning, my father severely challenged me with a litany of unpleasant and indeed, inaccurate innuendoes. It was, in fact, perfectly innocent, as I had gone to Rosemary's house after the movie for coffee, music, and conversation. The timing of my father's challenge was poor, he was in the wrong, and the lack of any future such accusations ensured the resulting embarrassment was never repeated. I was hurt and offended, by what I felt was a lack of trust in me by my father. As the oldest of my siblings, I was conceivably the experiment by which my parents would learn how to manage the rest of their children. As I was somewhat removed from my siblings by age, and eventually by distance, I have no idea if they did or not.

When Sami Leban, the Karachi InterContinental hotel's hairdresser and his girlfriend invite me to move into a spare room they had in their flat, I was happy to do so. To live with new friends helped ease the loneliness.

Sami, with whom I had become friendly, was not an employee of the InterContinental Hotel, but the leaseholder of the beauty salon, and his girlfriend was one of his stylists. Sami was Lebanese and I was to soon learn he was a little hot tempered. I moved out of their flat within a month. Too much hot-blooded clashing of testosterone and oestrogen between Sami and his girlfriend created an uncomfortable environment. I made the excuse that I had a better offer, and I hoped they would not be offended? They were not, and we continued our friendship. In fact, I did have a better offer, or so I thought at the time.

I moved into the home of the hotel's chief engineer, Khalid Butt, and his wife, Billo. They had a very large apartment close to the Beach Luxury hotel, with lots of space and no family. I had become friends with Khalid, hence the invitation. On one occasion Billo became an unexpected challenge when Khalid was away. Khalid was chief engineer for the three InterContinental hotels in Pakistan, and he travelled frequently. Billo was possibly in her mid thirties and it seemed may have liked younger men, that was the rumour at least. Late one evening, while she and I were alone in the house, she asked me to accompany her on a drive, ostensibly to purchase cigarettes. The drive's real purpose was less about cigarettes and more about dark, lonely places and sex. I resisted.

Not because when opportunity knocked I didn't always open the door, but I was careful, well, after my youthful daliance with my cousin at sixteen, I was always careful.

At sixteen I needed money and decided to go to England to work during the summer holidays. I persuaded my Father to ask his brother, my uncle Stephen to try and find me a job. He obliged and obtained a position for me as a clerk with a shipping company. He also offered to accommodate me in his home, in Dagenham Essex, which suited my father, relieving him of the worry of me staying with strangers.

While I knew the rest of my father's siblings, I never remembered meeting Uncle Stephen, probably because, unlike other members of my father's family who lived in England, Stephen had never returned to visit Ireland. Stephen's wife Kitty, was English. She seemed to me somewhat blousy, was a heavy smoker, continually watched soaps on TV, and seemed to shout at her children a lot.

Stephen was a projectionist at the local cinema, and he worked most evenings until quite late. This situation afforded their four children many opportunities to do their own thing, and they took advantage of that.

Ann was the eldest, about my age, I found myself attracted to her. Yes, she was my cousin, but I had never met her before or even knew of her existence. She was blonde, dressed and carried herself quite provocatively, and seemed more worldly than the Irish girls I knew then. I concluded, it must be because she was English and lived in London.

The scent of her perfume, the toss of her hair, the swish of her skirt, raised my desires and I knew I was threading a dangereous path, but I couldn't help myself. At sixteen my hormones were in control not I. As we were in the same house, all the circumstances converged to create the environment for a 'dangerous liaison'. We both just turned sixteen. Knowing glances across the dining room table and raging hormones threw caution to the wind; walks in the evening in the park, where shadows from the trees on moonlit nights hid our indiscretions. Intimate contact in Ann's room when no one was at home and we were finally lost in each others unstopable passion. That summer of nineteen fifty eight was the the summer of new experiences and new emotions. This was a very risky encounter however, because, if our parents ever found out there would be hell to pay, and the families scandalized. They never did, and at the end of that summer, I returned to Dublin secure in the knowledge the secret was buried, never to be mentioned. And it never was until now!

Quickly after the unexpected and shocked encounter with Billo, and for the last time while in Karachi, I once again moved, this time into a flat with an Irish couple I'd met at the St. Patrick's Day party I attended earlier in March. Felix and Ann were a middle-aged couple who probably felt protective toward the young Irishman thousands of miles from his homeland in a strange country, and they invited me to stay with them - an offer I gladly accepted.

Moving in and moving out was not a strange hobby I'd somehow acquired upon my arrival in Karachi, although it might seem so. New contacts were made, new acquaintances formed, and new events and customs experienced. I quickly adjusted to life so far from Ireland and what I was used to, and began to enjoy and appreciate the difference in lifestyle and culture. I learned to enjoy the heat, ignore the noise and the dust and get used to travelling around the city by auto rickshaw.

As Pauline's letters became less and less frequent, it became apparent that she might never join me, and about three months after my arrival in Karachi, I received the 'Dear John' letter confirming our relationship was over. Strangely enough, while it upset me, it did not do so to the extent I thought it might. In this instance, distance did not 'make the heart grow fonder'. I had become used to not having her company, was probably subconsciously expecting the breakup, and now felt a sense of freedom, as I had become very aware of the many attractive young women who populated the social space I often frequented.

A local girl who was a flight attendant with Pakistan International Airways----an exotic version of Adrienne, in whose company I had happily spent all evening at a St Patrick Day house party I'd attended in March, refused my invitation to dinner. "If we were in London, Paris, or Rome, I'd love to spend time with you Colm, but not here in Karachi in a public place. I'd be tarnished with a brush I don't wish for."

Thus was my introduction to the conservative culture I began to recognise as a separation of genders. However, while this existed in the sixties, it was less an issue than it later became with the rise of Islamic fundamentalism following the highly conservative presidency of Zia ul Hag during the seventies. His presidency sowed the seeds for the extreme social culture of present-day Pakistan.

Ignoring what I should have learned at that St. Patrick's day party, a few weeks later I succumbed to temption and asked Shahnaz a receptionist from the hotel, out for a drink. She accepted! On a beautiful, warm, moonlit evening, after work we strolled the short distance from the InterContinental Hotel to the nearby Palace Hotel. The Palace Hotel was an older property from the time of the Raj, it was well maintained and had an extensive garden bar. Unfortunately, this time, I experienced a more aggressive side of that conservative culture.

"What you doing with her?" a police officer enquired in fractured english as he approached our table.

"Having a drink. What's the problem?" I asked.

While there were several couples sitting at tables throughout the garden, I was the only white face to be seen. Maybe for me, the penny had not dropped yet, but it was in the slot.

"Leave now." He forcefully suggested, rather instructed!

I was both nervous and angry. This was my first encounter with law enforcement in a country I was as yet unfamiliar with. *What have I got myself into? It was just a drink with a girl in a hotel garden*, I naively thought.

Shahnaz was upset and in tears. She was a receptionist in the InterContinental hotel, a respectable and, indeed, envied position, requiring high levels of literacy and the ability to be fluent in several languages, including English. She explained that her father was a commodore in the Pakistani navy and she came from a good family, and now, with the implication from this police officer that she was involved in something less than honourable, her integrity was impeached.

Later, I wondered if that incident had just been seen by the police officer as an opportunity for a contribution to his 'personal pension fund'. I had been to clubs, bars, and hotels in Karachi where men and women intermingled without let or hindrance, so this incident initially seemed just a little strange to me. In time, it became apparent to me that what was acceptable in some locations or on some levels might not universally apply. After seeing Shahnaz off home in a auto rickshaw, I decided I would in the future focus my attention on Western girls, mostly daughters of expatriate parents. The separation of genders didn't seem to apply to foreigners, or maybe it was more about foreign men with Pakistani women, which was rare, more than it was about men and women together. The penny dropped!

"Colm, would you like to come to the yacht club with us on Sunday," Felix asked me one Saturday afternoon when I had been staying with them for about a month.

"We'll race our Enterprise 420s, and afterwards, have a nice curry lunch."

"Sure, I'd love to,".

Many years earlier, one of my friends in Mount Merrion Co.

Dublin, whom I met shortly after our family moved there in 1950, was John O'Connor. One day, when I was about ten years old, while playing outside on the street with John, we saw Captain Jack out in his front garden, which was overgrown with weeds and uncut grass. Although he only lived three or four houses from John, he was rarely seen. We knew he was a fisherman and owned a fishing trawler, which was berthed in Dun Laoire Harbour. We thought we didn't see him because he must be out at sea fishing on his trawler all the time.

"Let's say hello to Captain Jack and ask him if we could see his fishing boat one day," suggested John.

"We must be polite and say we hope he's catching lots of fish."

We approached him. John breathlessly asked,

"Hello, Captain Jack. I hope you're catching lots of fish. Can we see your fishing boat some time?"

We were surprised by the immediate response from Captain Jack:

"Sure. I'm going there this afternoon. If you'd like to come, check with your parents and ask them to let me know if it's okay."

Excited, we ran home, received the required approval, and set off for Dun Laoire with Captain Jack that afternoon. While his car was a rickety old rust bucket that slowly rattled its way to its destination, his boat was quite something special. It was absolutely pristine. *This is the most beautiful thing I have ever seen*, was my immediate thought. The hull and doghouse were marine navy blue with mirror-finish paintwork that sparkled like the shimmering sea itself. The cap rail and wood trim had a varnish so deep it was almost three-dimensional. The naturally weathered teak decks were immaculate, and the brass work glistened like gold reflecting the sky and the sun. We wandered the deck but never got to go inside. Later, I said to John.

"I suppose he didn't want us kids dirtying up his carpets and upholstery."

It was indeed a fishing trawler, but the decks had probably never seen fish, and Captain Jack was not actually a fisherman. He was a lover of the sea and of boats.

That cold, windy afternoon on Captain Jack's boat was when I too fell in love with boats and the sea. As I looked out over the Irish Sea, with the waves building and the white crests crashing over again and again, I felt a rush of excitement, I began to dream. I never lost that love of the sea and of sailing. Sailing became my mistress, my passion, and I continued to sail during most of the rest of my life. I loved the varied moods of the ocean. I loved being on the water with white sails billowing in the breeze, silently carrying the boat across the azure water, as white clouds drift across a blue sky, or, when the weather was angry with grey black clouds low and heavy in the sky, and vicious winds screaming through the boat's rigging. Glorious nature at it's purest!

Since my childhood encounter with Captain Jack, I had dreamed of a moment like this, and now in Karachi, here was an opportunity to realise that dream.

I went that Sunday in early May and continued to do so most Sundays for the remaining time I spent in Karachi. The yacht club was on an small island in Karachi harbour, and we would take the club tender over early Sunday mornings. I loved the weekly regattas, was an eager student, and became quite a competent sailor. I also enjoyed the social aspect the vast majority of the time. However, I would occasionally feel a sense of discomfort with what I thought of as a pseudo-colonial attitude that sometimes seemed to pervade the club's atmosphere, which was almost entirely frequented by white career expatriate British families, with a smattering of Pakistani elite. I was young, single, Irish, and atypical of the club membership. I'd made several local acquaintances through introductions by Sami Leban, and to some extent, was more comfortable with them than with the expatriate yacht club crowd. Feeling as I did, it was around this time I concluded that in the future, I would integrate into whatever local community I lived and avoid the expatriate brigade.

In early May, I received a phone call at work one morning. "Is that Colm Madden?" the voice on the other end of the telephone line asked.

"Yes. That's me."

"Colm, this is Monsignor Dolan from the papal nunciature embassy in Clifton". Clifton was a popular residential suburb of Karachi, right on the coast and often frequented by evening walkers and families enjoying the sea air as they strolled along the shoreline.

"I know your father, and if you're free one evening, I'd like to invite you to the embassy for dinner."

Although the capital of Pakistan had moved from Karachi to Islamabad the year before in 1965, the papal nunciature did not move until later in 1967.

I was rather surprised with this call out of the blue. My father had never indicated that he knew anyone in Karachi or any other papal nunciature staff elsewhere for that matter. I mumbled through my response: "Any evening would be fine."

"How about Friday around seven p.m.? I'll send a car for you. Just give me your address."

"I look forward to it," I lied as I provided the address.

I'd much rather spend my evenings with some of the young people I knew. The Beach Luxury Hotel was located close the shoreline in a residental suburb of Karachi and the bar there was one favourite hangout for the crowd that I had become friendly with. After meeting there on a Friday or Saturday night, following preliminary drinks, we would go on to restaurants and frequently to cabarets.

That was much more interesting than having dinner with some elderly priest. I didn't understand why this invitation was forthcoming. Monsignor Dolan had said he knew my father, and that was apparently the reason; after all, I was just a department head at the InterContinental Hotel in Karachi, hardly the usual candidate for an invitation to the papal nuncio's for dinner! *Anyway, I'd better go now that I've accepted the invitation, and he knows my father*, not really looking forward to the occasion. Years later, I concluded that my father probably did not, in fact, know Monsignor Dolan, but had covertly been in contact with the nunciature in order to ensure I was 'religiously supervised'.

It was Tuesday, still the best part of the week to go, before the papal nunciature dinner, and I was very busy. In those days, Karachi InterContinental Hotel was constantly close to hundred percent occupancy, and being one of the busiest hotels in the company, the laundry always operated at maximum capacity. Malik, my assistant manager, was a hard worker, a competent supervisor, and a good intermediary between the staff and myself. Apart from the different languages, ethnicity, and the absence of female staff, the laundry was a carbon copy of the one in Dublin, and very likely, it was much the same as those in the other sixty or seventy InterContinental Hotels around the world. As expected of any hotel in a renowned international chain, all the latest equipment was in place, but still, it was labour-intensive work, and the ability to manage and motivate people was the key to an effective operation, a skill at which I was becoming very accomplished and for which I would be recognised throughout my career.

Friday evening arrived, and at seven pm, a diplomatic car stopped outside Felix and Ann's flat.

"Colm there's a car here for you," Ann called out.

"On my way" .

I'd told them that I was off to the papal nunciature for dinner.

"Moving in diplomatic circles already, I see," joked Ann.

At the door of the embassy, Monsignor Dolan greeted me.

He's only a young man, much younger than I expected for a monsignor and presumably accomplished in international and church diplomacy. I began to feel better that I didn't have to suffer through dinner with some 'old fossil', an uncharitable and unkindly description that had occurred to me.

"Would you like a drink, Colm? I'm having a Campari and soda."

"Sure, I'll have the same." *This is not so bad. Seems like a nice guy, and I get to have a drink or two and a nice dinner.*

As the evening wore on, in spite of my earlier reservations, I enjoyed myself. Monsignor Dolan was pleasant company, the dinner was excellent, and we shared a bottle of good wine and after-dinner brandies. The conversation was easy, centring on how I was settling into life in Karachi, how my job was going, and a little about each other's backgrounds and families. As I was departing some four hours later, with a warm glow of contentment and satisfaction, Monsignor Dolan extended an invitation again for the following Friday evening. I happily accepted. Friday night dinner became a frequent event I looked forward to, and Monsignor Dolan and I became friends. On one occasion, I met the papal nuncio, Archbishop Saverio Zupi, who joined us for a glass of wine.

One day in early May of 1966, the laundry clerk came out from the office and onto the laundry floor.

"Colm sahib, Mr Stouffer's secretary is on the phone in the office."

"Okay, I'm coming."

"Colm, Mr Stouffer would like to invite you to join them for the beach picnic on Sunday."

"Great, I look forward to it".

Stouffer was the hotel general manager, and it was a tradition to invite expatriate staff to join him and his family at the hotel's beach house on Sandspit beach each Sunday. Sandspit was a popular beach for the elite of Karachi. Many well off locals had beach houses there and would spend their free time enjoying the sun, sand and sea. The less well off tended to use Hawksbay which was nearer the city. This invitation was rotated and would be repeated every month or two. Some invitees were more frequent guests than others, such as the resident manager, Mr Herrera, his wife, and their 'twenty-something' daughter, Anita. Although I had now been at the hotel for four months, this was my first beach party invitation. These Sunday parties were lavish affairs and only the best wines, champagne, and other adult beverages were provided, along with an extensive range of food of the very highest standard, prepared in advance in the hotel kitchens. Staff worked a six-day week, and while I worked a normal workday because my department operated daytime hours, many of my colleagues in food and beverage and the rooms division worked long hours, frequently late into the night. Sunday was the one day available for relaxation and enjoyment, and it was certainly taken advantage of.

The Sunday I was invited; there were about a dozen others there, including Anita. She and I struck up a conversation, and the chemistry was there, attraction and opportunity. The warmth of the sunshine, an inner glow from the champagne, and the lapping blue sea on the shore, as we sat side by side on a rug on the sand in intimate conversation, created an atmosphere where romance might blossom. Anita was tender, soft spoken and very attractively 'South American'. I loved the exotic!

"Have dinner with me?" I asked. She agreed, and we dined in the InterContinental Hotel's rooftop restaurant the following evening. The mood was romantic as we sat at a window table, as the lights of the city twinkled below us, while the Italian band played soft music. We danced, we spent hours over dinner enjoying easy conversation, good food and companionship. We strolled around the hotel gardens after dinner, late into the night, content in each other's company. We kissed! We were beginning to develop a warm relationship, and were together as often as both time and discretion would permit. Being the daughter of my boss was a situation that required careful handling, particularly in the hotel business, where frequently the lines between work and private life are blurred. However, our sands of time together were quickly running out.

Early in September, I received a call in my office from Ellen, the general manager's secretary.

"Colm, can you come to Mr Stouffer's office, please?"

"Sure, is there a problem?"

"I don't believe so," replied Ellen. "He has Tex Stovall, corporate director of laundries, who just arrived from the US, with him."

I had never met Stovall, and wondered why he was here in Karachi, what he was like, and what this summons was about as I made my way to the executive offices.

"Go on in. They're expecting you," greeted Ellen.

"Hello, Colm. I don't believe you've met Mr Stovall."

"Please, call me Tex," Stovall immediately responded. He was a big man, over sixty years of age, with white hair styled in a crew cut. I later learned that he was a former marine, which may have accounted for his straight-as-a-die posture and his apparently fit physique.

"Colm, I understand from Mr Stouffer that you've done an excellent job here in managing your department and developing the staff. How do you feel that your assistant is in terms of management skills?" Tex asked.

I wondered where this was leading. Somewhere for sure—it wasn't just idle conversation!

"Malik is doing well, I'm happy with his ability, and he has been very helpful to me."

"If we had something new for you, would he be ready to take over as the department manager?" Stouffer enquired.

"Yes, with a little additional training on procedural issues. His technical and people-management skills are strong, and the staff like and respect him".

"Can you get him ready in one month?" Stovall asked.

I was now at the point in the conversation where I needed to know its direction.

"Can I ask what this is about?"

"Yes of course," said Stovall. "We'd like to transfer you to Dacca, East Pakistan, to set up the laundry for the new hotel opening soon. You've done a good job here, and we want you to do this opening. It'll be a good experience for you."

So, that was it, a transfer to Dacca, East Pakistan, considered by many of the foreign staff in the Karachi hotel as the place not to go to, a backwater with nothing to do and nowhere to go outside of the upcoming InterContinental Hotel. This was to be the first hotel of any significance in East Pakistan, the poor, deprived, and believed by many Bengalis (natives of the region of Bengal, of which East Bengal was East Pakistan and West Bengal was a state in India) to be the 'plundered' other half of this impoverished country. I did not relish the idea, but knew I had little choice. I'd been with the company for less than a year. They told me I was doing a good job, offered me the opportunity to participate in an opening, and virtually suggested it would probably be a good idea to accept. I had only one option!

"I can have Malik ready in a month with a push,", and I did. In the last week of September 1966, Malik was promoted to laundry manager at the Karachi InterContinental Hotel.

I left the meeting with Stovall and Stouffer that day extremely apprehensive. I knew nothing of East Pakistan, other than what I'd heard around the hotel from others. Somewhat backwards seemed to be the commonly held belief. Of course, I'd known nothing of West Pakistan before I arrived in Karachi either

I was also ambivalent about my relationship with Anita; was it just a fleeting moment, a passing fancy? I liked her and loved being with her, but I knew I was not in love with her. I had loved Pauline and the feeling was different. Yet I was going to a place where I might remain for several years without female companionship. Yes, that concerned me! I related well socially to female friends and companions. And I was young, I needed their company. Should I ask if she would come with me? I called her.

"Hi Anita, can you meet me in the lobby bar this evening after work"

"Sure what time?"

"Around six."

"Okay, see you then."

The lobby bar was noisy, busy with the end of the work day drinkers, as Anita arrived, looking pretty, and stylishly dressed, as she always did.

"What would you like to drink?"

"White wine please Colm. What's up? You have a sort of concerned look about you."

"Bad news I' afraid. I'm being transferred to Dacca"

"What! When is this happening?".

"Beginning of October. I'd like to ask you something. I know it's really a big step, but, would you consider coming with me?"

"I can't think about that now" was her curt response. Her eyes welled up and tears began to build. I was lost for how to console her as she quickly departed the bar. The noisy bar was not the place to attempt to talk our way through the raw emotions we now felt, and I probably should have sought a quieter location.

While I hoped she would consider coming with me to Dacca, my instinct was, she would decline. We had so little time together and yet the joy we had experienced was now to be ripped from us. I momentarily resented the Company's decision to move me to Dacca.

I knew she had rejected the advances of Victor Lima, the hotel's front office manager, in favour of me. They'd known each other for a long time even before Karachi, when they'd lived in Uruquay, their home country. I knew that Victor was a safety net, as was staying with her parents in Karachi. I was offering risk, Dacca, and the unknown. She eventually turned down my invitation, and after that evening, we spent no further time together. After October I never saw her again,. Years later, I learned that Anita and Victor Lima had married.

On the very day I was due to leave for Dacca, a key core group of the new Dacca hotel staff arrived for training in Karachi. They toured the hotel and my attention was drawn to one young lady in the group, named Shelley RajLaxmi Roy Paladhy. I found her striking, and was immediately drawn to her, like a moth to a flame. She was petite, with big, dark eyes, infectious laughter and a smile that could light up, not only a room, but a whole house with joy. Instantly, I felt I needed to know her, like no one I'd known before.

That same evening in early October 1966, I left Karachi on the two hour flight to Dacca, East Pakistan, and my new assignment. It was my first opportunity to be involved in the opening of a hotel and the start-up of a new business. It was an exciting prospect, and although I was apprehensive and hoped I was up to the task, I began to look forward to it.

Shelley

Colm

Chapter Two

Dacca, East Pakistan

The PIA flight from Karachi landed at Dacca airport following a two-hour journey. Suleman Aidenwalla, the assistant front office manager in the Karachi InterContinental who had now been promoted to front office manager for the Dacca InterContinental Hotel was also on the same flight. He and I were the only transferees from Karachi, while the rest of the Dacca management team were expatriates from other InterContinental Hotels around the world, supported by some locally hired managers.

As I disembarked onto East Pakistan's fertile soil, my senses were overwhelmed by the emerald greenness of the tropical growth and, unfortunately, the weight of the humidity, which hung like a warm, wet blanket around me. The temperature may have been slightly lower than Karachi's, but it felt hotter, and I was soon soaked in perspiration. The monsoons had ended, yet the moisture still hung heavy in the air.

The hotel driver, a short jolly fellow, along with a new locally appointed duty manager Charles, greeted us at the airport and quickly collecting our luggage, ushered us into the air-conditioned comfort of the hotel's minibus, which eventually brought us to a rather large old house within walking distance from the

InterContinental Hotel. The company had rented it on a temporary basis, to accommodate incoming expatriate staff. The house was not in the best condition, behind an unkempt wall of scrub bushes, trees, weeds and tall grass. It was dark, semi derelict and reminiscent of a 'haunted house' from a movie or TV show, but the availability of anything more luxurious for rent in Dacca might have been slim. The expatriate staff would eventually be assigned accommodation in the hotel upon completion of the guest rooms.

Following the hustle and the bustle of Karachi, Dacca more resembled a provincial town, albeit a large one, than the regional capital of what was then East Pakistan, later to become Bangladesh. With a population around two and a half million, it was smaller and less crowded than Karachi. In subsequent years, however, Dacca would become one of the world's fastest-growing, most densely populated cities, and half a century later, it supports a population around fourteen million souls. After the desert-like landscape surrounding Karachi, the lush emerald green of tropical East Pakistan with its bright green paddy fields, its multitude of palm tree ringed ponds and its leafy plants and grasses was pleasantly soothing to the eye.

The opening of the Dacca InterContinental Hotel, of similar size and architectural style to the Karachi hotel, was scheduled for about eight weeks hence, and there were several expatriate managers already onsite involved in pre-opening activities. Their respective roles determined the amount of time each needed to be on board prior to opening. Construction, development, procurement, and engineering staff who had been involved from the beginning had been in Dacca for a couple of years. Construction work was still very much in progress and would continue so right up until a day or two before opening, with workers everywhere scurrying about like ants on an anthill.

Each department head was responsible for ensuring that the development and procurement staff provided for the needs of their individual departments. The lobbying was intense and on occasion, led to some degree of friction as operations managers fought to have their individual needs be a top priority. I was no exception, and as this was my first hotel opening, I was enthusiastically learning the ropes.

I became friendly with Ray O'Shea, the corporate procurement manager who was part of the 'pre-opening,' team, and we frequently socialised together after work. Ray was very helpful to me in getting ready for the big event. Approximately three weeks prior to opening, the big old house was vacated, the corporate pre-opening staff left Dacca, and the expatriate operational staff moved into the hotel. As a five-star property, the guest rooms were very comfortable, but living in the place where one worked was hardly conducive to the protection of one's private life, as I would eventually discover.

There were approximately five hundred jobs on offer at the first international hotel in East Pakistan, and as they were considered prime positions, with opportunities never before available, thousands applied. Managing the constant hordes of applicants for interviews was challenging. The hotel ballroom was used as a preliminary screening centre, and all department managers, assistant managers, and other expatriate and local management staff had already been enlisted as screeners. They referred potential candidates to the human resources department for final approval. Those approved and appropriately qualified were then interviewed by the management of the department they had applied for, and the lucky ones selected.

I had about fifty new employees in my department, and not a single one had any experience with the methods, equipment, or technology of modern laundry and dry-cleaning systems, so the training task ahead was to become monumental. Tex Stovall, the IHC corporate director of laundries whom I had met earlier in Karachi, was on site, and he and I began the training process. In spite of their lack of experience, the new employees were enthusiastic. They learned quickly and were ready in time for the big day.

The hotel opened to much fanfare towards the end of 1966, and I had participated in my first opening,. Guests arrived and were serviced by enthusiastic, well-trained, and friendly staff who were eager to please and proud of their new hotel, a beacon of modernity in this relatively underdeveloped region. My staff performed well 'under fire,' and we were off to an effective and efficient beginning.

Being young and single and presumed, at least by some, to be a somewhat eligible bachelor, my affections were targeted by one of the older duty managers as a potential candidate to 'rescue' his daughter, hopefully marry her, and bring her to Britain, where she rightfully belonged. Charles, who originally met us at the airport, and his family were Anglo-Indians, who became Pakistani citizens. Their ancestors had intermarried with British colonials during the Raj, and many of their descendants were conflicted between their Indian and British heritage. Some, though living on the subcontinent for generations, had never totally integrated into its society and in a way, were culturally lost somewhere between Britain and India or Pakistan.

I was not interested, remembering Shelley, who had visited Karachi earlier on a familiarisation tour and who'd had an immediate impact on me. Somehow I felt connected to her to the exclusion of others, and if one where to believe in reincarnation, as I was to learn she did, than maybe a past life intertwined us. She was now working in her new position at the reception desk.

By now, I was quite familiar with the cultural issues surrounding such romantic liaisons, having on two occasions in Karachi experienced what I thought of as the separation of genders. I had fallen for Shelley, and maybe a romantic notion, but yes, it was love at first sight. I was hopeful we could have a relationship, but I was insecure and unsure how to broach the subject with her, given my earlier experiences in Karachi. While I considered approaching her several times, I never did so, 'chickening out' at the last minute fearful of rejection. Eventually, I decided to enlist some help and made my feelings known to two of my colleagues, Suleman Adenwalla, the front office manager and RajLaxmi's boss, and S. Haqqi, the banquet manager. Haqqi had known Shelley before joining the InterContinental Hotel, so he said he'd be happy to intercede.

Shortly after the hotel opening, Haqqi came to my office.

"Ok, Colm, we're going out for dinner tonight."

"We are, how come?" .

"We have a date, three of us, you, me. and Shelley."

I was surprised, but pleased that Haqqi had asked and Shelley had agreed. I knew the occasion might be a little strained—after all 'three is a crowd'—and while I had spoken to Shelley at work, and took every opportunity to do so, this would 'break the ice' on a personal level. It would have been easier if it was just 'dinner for two'; however, I knew that Haqqi being there would overcome my concern about me, a European male being alone with a local girl.

My relationship with Shelley developed in a way that might have been more akin to old-fashioned courting rather than what would be considered the Western idea of dating. The culture challenged the idea of going to dances, bars, and restaurants or for walks alone together, and for that reason, much of our time was spent at Shelley's home. Before first visiting her home and meeting her family, she and I managed a few discreet dates, and I also experienced a few unavailables. Shelley was understandably unsure of my intentions. I was a young, single foreign man far away from home. How would she know the purpose or outcome of such a relationship?

On one occasion, there was a particularly creative test of my sincerity. We had agreed to meet one evening and go to the

Daffodil Hotel for drinks. The hotel was a small property within walking distance of the InterContinental Hotel. It had four or five guest rooms, a small basic restaurant, and a bar. Not many customers frequented the pleasant garden, where we could sit out and enjoy an evening without being scrutinised. At the time appointed to meet me outside the InterContinental Hotel, Shelley's car arrived with her driver, but without her. The driver alighted from the car and handed me a carton of cigarettes, I smoked in those days, with a note taped to it. Then he got back in the car and drove away. The note said "I'm very sorry I can't make it tonight," with no further explanation! I wondered, *Is this the brush off?*

Following that incident, however, my attention to Shelley continued to demonstrate my sincerity, and our relationship grew. It became a regular routine for me to finish my evening meal in the hotel and, afterwards, visit Shelley at her home. Occasionally, we would go out to a restaurant or to the movies, but usually, went with groups or family members; it was easier considering the cultural issues. I was readily accepted by family and friends and participated in several family events.

In December of 1966, I asked Shelley to marry me, and she said yes. I had been rather careless about communicating with my parents in Ireland, and it was about three months since I had last written home. It was long before the advent of the 'information highway', as the internet was first called; therefore, the convenience of emailing was unavailable. Telephoning might have been an option, but the service was poor, and the cost was excessive. However, it was important to advise them of the decision I had taken, so I set about writing the long-overdue letter with what I knew would be controversial information. With Shelley being a Hindu and I a Catholic, I was sure the religious difference would be an issue, especially with my father. I wondered if there would be a racial issue also, adding another crack in our fractured relationship? With little exposure to other races in Ireland of the sixties, where pennies were collected in schools and churches for the 'black babies' in Africa, there existed a sort of benign mild racism.

I didn't really feel close to my father. Notwithstanding our earlier disagreements, maybe what I also learned about my father during my teenage years and it's impact on me, was one more factor in growing the distance that seperated us?

I learned of his personal anguish, his lost dream of returning to America, where he'd spent several years during the 1930s. While my father would never say so, I believe, that since he now had a family he was unwilling to take them to America because he feared the possibility of failure. So he chose to be unhappily secure rather than courageously adventerous. I never understood why that was, since the nineteen fifties was boom time in the USA. His dislike bordering on hatred for his job, and his frustration at always being passed over for promotion and denied benefits he felt were due to him, was difficult for me to come to terms with. I knew how he felt, as he frequently expressed those feelings. His involvement with the Commercial Traveller Federation, the 'union' for sales representatives, and his position on their executive board might have been largely due to his view of his work life, and the corporate culture that gave him a living, yet also demoralised him. This had a profound impact on me. Somehow, either instinctively or subconsciously, it shaped my thinking and became a model of how I was not willing to live my own life. It is said we learn by example, what to do, but surely also, what not to do. How not to live my own life was one of the most profound and lasting lessons I learned from my father, and it has shaped much of my view of work and of life. Unfortunately there was an unwanted dimension to these lessons. It was the diminution of respect I had for my father. I loved him, he was a good man, a good provider for his family, but I felt, maybe unjustly so, that he walked a cowardly path. If he wanted to go to America, why didn't he? If he hated his job why not change it, others have done so, others with families also? I hated how I felt, but couldn't shake those thoughts and feelings.

Being on another continent thousands of miles from home didn't make communication easier. Mail usually took a couple of week each way, so until the reply to my letter arrived the tension was palpable. Early in January 1967, I received the much-awaited letter from my father, and it was certainly not what I had hoped for, but it was not entirely unexpected. I could not imagine what mental picture my father had conjured up of the situation or of Shelley, but the letter contained several unpleasant innuendos along with the suggestion, "If you got the girl pregnant, then leave the country," supported by several other disturbing comments.

Shortly after I received this letter, I also got a phone call from Monsignor Dolan from Karachi.

"Colm, your father contacted me to ask for my assistance. He says you've become involved with a local Hindu girl. I think this is a bad idea," to paraphrase.

This conversation eventually deteriorated to the point where I suggested it was none of Monsignor Dolan's business. It was both an unpleasant and, indeed, unhappy occasion.

The letter from my father and the call from him to Monsignor Dolan, who I believed had become my friend, where two more incidents that chipped away at the deteriorating relationship between father and son.

It became apparent that in Ireland, my news was a serious topic in the family home. But I did receive support from my maternal grandmother and my youngest, sixteen-year-old sister, who undoubtedly nutured romantic, exotic notions.

I had not expected quite such a strong reaction from my father, but buoyed by support from other family members, I was determined to put the situation right. I decided to write, enclosing a picture of Shelley and more details of her and her family.

Subsequently, Shelley also wrote to my family, and eventually, a response to both letters was received from Ireland wishing us long life and happiness. Maybe reluctant acceptance, but it was there and we were elated, the first hurdle was overcome. But it was touched by a note of sadness, as my friendship with Monsignor Dolan was irreparably damaged, and we never again spoke.

Shelley's father had passed away when she was about thirteen years of age, and her mother, brothers, and sisters were quite liberal by local standards. They already knew me, and had no issues with our decision to marry. Shelley's earlier career as a flight attendant, flying throughout Europe and the USA, had broadened her own outlook and experience, so between she and I, cultural barriers were non existant.

In the 1960s, regardless of how liberal young people thought they were, in Ireland, there continued to be a strong connection to the traditions of the Catholic Church, of which I was a member. I therefore wanted to have a church wedding, and in those days, with a Hindu bride, this posed a challenge. I approached the local parish priest, an American on secondment to the diocese of Dacca to provide for the spiritual wellbeing of local and expatriate Catholics. Father Zimmerman was not initially hopeful he could help. A Church dispensation was required, and he advised the young couple that the archbishop in Dacca was unlikely to forward a request to the Vatican, as he was opposed to mixed marriages. Shelley volunteered to convert, but I was not in favour of such action just for the sake of expediency. After continuous visits from me, Father Zimmerman eventually succumbed to my persistence and offered to contact the archbishop of Bangkok, Thailand, who quite frequently supported dispensations. A positive response was duly received, and plans were made to fly to Bangkok to be married.

On April 3, 1967, Shelley and I were on a flight from Dacca to Bangkok. This flight immediately followed PIA's maiden flight on that route on April 2, and strangely enough, we were the only passengers on board. Clearing customs and immigration at Bangkok Airport, we took a taxi to the Siam InterContinental Hotel, and that evening, dined with Tex Stovall, who had timed his visit to Bangkok to coincide with the wedding. The following day, we met with Father Tan at Assumption Cathedral and arranged to return the next morning to be married.

Early on April 5, 1967, along with our two witnesses, we returned to the cathedral for the ceremony. It was a simple affair, in Father Tan's living room while sitting on his sofa, and it took all of ten minutes. The marriage was approved and recognised by the Catholic Church, but the sacrament of Matrimony was not administered because of the religious difference.

As a newly married couple we spent the next five days in Bangkok on honeymoon, enjoying the city, its many historical sights, and the incredible array of Buddhist temples, including the Jade Buddha, the enormous Reclining Buddha, and the Golden Buddha, along with other unique attractions. Nightlife in Bangkok at the time was a booming and eye-opening industry. The Vietnam War was still raging, and this city was a favourite destination for a continuous stream of American troops on leave. This created an opportunity for those Thais with a liberal outlook on life to tap into the pockets of free-spending soldiers out for a good time away from the horrors of war.

One night, Shelley and I visited one of the more popular nightclubs, very upmarket, elegant, and expensive. Inside the main area of the club, one wall was completely glass, fronting a large, sumptuously furnished lounge where several dozen very attractive, elegantly dressed young ladies were seated, all supporting numbered tags attached to their clothing. Any male client of the club who wished, could identify by number a young lady he wanted to spend time with, either dancing or just sitting in conversation. More young ladies were in the general area of the club, either dancing or sitting at tables with a variety of male companions, mostly American soldiers. To me, it conjured up a vision of what it might have been like, though considerably less elegant in the American dance halls during the Great Depression, later immortalised in Tina Turner's song "Private Dancer".

One week following our arrival in Bangkok, we returned to Dacca a married couple. Since the wedding itself had been such a simple affair, it was considered appropriate to greet friends and family as Mr and Mrs Madden, so we organised a reception to take place a month after the wedding. Little organisation was actually required other than sending invitations, as the event was to be held in the InterContinental Hotel for a small group of about fifty.

We moved into our first home, a tiny cottage in a nice residential area of Dacca, with a total area of about 300 square feet consisting of one tiny bedroom, an equally tiny living room, a dining area large enough for a small table and two chairs, a small bathroom, and an outside kitchen. To refer to the front of the cottage as a garden would have been a misnomer and a disservice to gardens everywhere. There was a tiny front yard behind the wrought-iron entrance gates, which contained a considerable number of pretty potted plants and flowers. We also bought the furniture that was in the cottage and kept the servants: a gardener, a cleaner, a cook, and a cook's helper. It was rather a lot of help for such a tiny cottage and just two young people, but as the staff had been with the previous tenants for several years, it helped us, as we had no talent for cooking or housekeeping.

Marshal, the cook, was a master in the kitchen and served up excellent food. He would go to the market in the morning and prepare breakfast, lunch, and dinner daily, and as the kitchen was outside the house, he would lock it each evening before going home. Shortly after moving into the cottage, one night while asleep in bed, we were awakened by a loud din coming from the kitchen. We could hear pots and pans crashing against the walls and falling on the floor. This went on for several minutes, and since Marshal was the only one with the kitchen keys, we were unable to investigate. Our first thoughts were maybe it was a cat, but since the kitchen only had a small screened window, that seemed unlikely. Next morning, when Marshal arrived to prepare breakfast, we saw the mess: pots, pans, and utensils strewn everywhere, with no evidence of a cat, rat, or other creature that might have wrought such havoc. When Marshal was asked for his opinion on what might have transpired, he strangely avoided the question and proposed no answer.

Several nights later, the scenario was again repeated around the same time. Again, Marshal avoided a response to the question. On a third occasion a couple of weeks later, this happened again, and then I was determined to find out what was going on. "Marshall, these occurrences in the kitchen don't seem to me to be normal, but you seem to accept them. You arrive in the mornings, tidy up the mess, go about your work, and don't express an opinion on what's happened when we ask you. If you know something about these disturbances, I want you to tell me now, and I insist you do so."

Here is Marshall's explanation, to paraphrase: "Many years ago, long before the cottage was built and this part of Dacca suburb was still countryside, there was a dirt path from one small hamlet to a second one. This path ran directly through the centre of what is now the kitchen, and a little further on to the side of this path, a tree grew where the bathroom is now located. A man from the first hamlet would regularly walk between the two hamlets late at night for some unknown, but what appeared to be a nefarious, purpose. One night, whatever trouble he was in overcame him, and as he walked the path through where the kitchen is, toward the tree where the bathroom is, he determined to end his anguish and hanged himself from that tree. So now his ghost will take that same walk from time to time, and as he walks through the shelves holding the pots and pans, they scatter, and hence the din. It's happened many times during the years I've worked here."

I was incredulous, and while tending to discount this story, it was devoid of another explanation. Some few weeks later, we invited our friends Chippy and his, wife Nelofer, over to the cottage one night for dinner, drinks, and to wait out late into the night to see if somehow we could encounter this elusive spirit. Chippy had recounted the story of other friends of his whose house was invaded by a ghost and who decided the best way to exorcise it was to talk to it nicely, asking it to please leave their home as it was disrupting their lives. According to Chippy, this worked, and the ghost never again bothered them.

On the night in question, the dinner was eaten, the company was enjoyable, and the adult beverage was flowing. The ladies didn't drink, but Chippy's and my excuse was that we were building up "Dutch Courage" in the event we encountered the ghost. We didn't, and the evening ended with both of us sufficiently inebriated that even if we had met this spirit, we were probably now incapable of stringing together a coherent enough request to encourage said ghost to depart the cottage.

Shelley became pregnant, and on one occasion, Indian Deputy High Commissioner Ashok Roy and his wife, Gautri, who were based in Dacca and knew the family, came to the cottage to congratulate Shelley and I on our marriage and subsequent pregnancy. They came in the official High Commission car, Indian flag flying, and parked outside the cottage. As it was daytime, the car was, of course, visible to neighbours and passers-by. Shortly after that visit, we had another one, this time from the Pakistani CID (central intelligence division). At that time, the relationship between Pakistan and India was tenuous at best, due to continuing hostilities over Kashmir. With Shelley's family being Brahmin Hindus originally from Kolkata and I a foreigner, the authorities viewed with some suspicion apparently, the visit to our home from the Indian deputy high commissioner. We were questioned for some time, but the responses were satisfactory, and the investigators departed, and that was the end of the matter, or so we thought.

Sometime later, the Indian High Commissioner Mr. Sen, whom Shelley also knew, came from Islamabad to Dacca for his farewell function, as he was being transferred out of Pakistan. Shelley and I were invited to this function, but while others received the invitations, we did not. Somehow, the invitations were suspiciously hijacked en route.

As Shelley's pregnancy advanced, we decided to give up the cottage and move into the Roy-Paladhy family home, where help and support would be readily available from mother and sisters. One late evening in mid-January 1968, we were out for a drive, and while driving along, enjoying the pleasant evening air, the car hit a large pothole in the road, and Shelley bounced high off her seat, returning with a thud. We were concerned for the baby, who promptly must have decided that she didn't enjoy these bumpy rides.

Around noon the following day, January 13, 1968, our daughter was born, weighing nine pounds four ounces. In due course, she was christened Erika Oona. She was a precious gift, a strong healthy baby, a life that as her father it was my responsibility to protect and ensure she was kept safe. As my own father had protected me as a baby.

When I was about one year old, I contracted diphtheria, and while on the way to the hospital, in the process of suffocating, my father continually poured glycerine down my throat in the hope of keeping my airways cleared. There was a major outbreak of diphtheria in Europe that year—fifty-thousand people, mostly children, died—and the 'Strangling Angel of Death' as the sickness was appropriatly named, struck down many children in Ireland also.

My contract included paid home leave after two years for myself and my family. Two years had now passed since my arrival in Pakistan and home leave was due. When Erika was two months old, the three of us flew to Karachi, where Erika would remain with Shelley's sister while Shelley and I flew on to Ireland.

While correspondence between my parents and I had become more frequent since Shelley and I were married and indeed between Shelley and my parents also, the prospect of meeting was ever so slightly daunting. The infamous letter from my father though not forgotten by me, was pushed to the 'back burner' and relationships improved. Shelley was not impacted by my relationship with my father, being unaware of earlier tensions between us. We were welcomed into the family home in Stillorgan by my parents. I was proud of my wife, her generosity of heart, the warmth of her spirit and her infectious smile and laughter quickly won over all my family. This included my father, who over time came to love her as his own daughter, and for that I loved him, notwithstanding the fact that he tried unsuccessfully over the years to convert her to Catholisism. A party was held and a housefull of aunts, uncles, and cousins came to meet us.

Following our two week leave we returned to Karachi, collected Erika, and returned to Dacca, the InterContinental Hotel, and work.

Unfolding political events in the country soon encroached upon the normalcy of our lives.

In 1966 Mujibur Rahman, leader of the East Pakistan chapter of the Awami League, proposed reforms, both economic and political for provincial autonomy. He believed that the central government, which was currently in West Pakistan, should be federal with its members elected on the basis of population. It would be responsible for defence and foreign affairs only. Both the east and west provinces, would have their own financial management. Each region could control its own earning of foreign exchange, and raise its own police and militia forces The central government would be funded from taxation collected at the provincial level.. This to provide a fair share of economic development for East Pakistan, which was seen by its people as unfairly treated by the existing central government and political system.

This was contrary to Pakistani President Ayub Khan's plan for full integration, which were shared by many West Pakistanis. They feared that Mujibur's proposal would divide the country by encouraging ethnic separation in West Pakistan, where a greater number of ethnic groups existed in contrast to East Pakistan, with its singularly Bengali ethnic population, which would be by far the greater and more powerful of the federating units.

Ayub saw Mujibur's demands as a move for independence. After pro-Mujibur supporters rioted in a general strike in Dhaka, the government arrested Mujibur in January 1968. This set the scene in East Pakistan for great anger towards the central government in the Western Province and was to lead to an increase in civil unrest later that year. A state of anarchy reigned, with protests and strikes throughout the country. The police appeared helpless to control the mob violence as unrest in the Eastern Province became rampant. Curfews were imposed throughout East Pakistan, and army units constantly patrolled the streets of Dacca.

For me and others at the hotel, evidence of the deployment of troops on the streets of Dacca came one morning when I heard that outside the InterContinental Hotel, on the main road from the army cantonment area to the city, soldiers were on the march. Curiosity prevailed, and several people, including myself, made our way to the front of the hotel only to see hundreds of heavily armed troops marching into the city centre. It was an ominous sign of things to come. With curfews now imposed, essential services were issued travel permits, and I was given one as the InterContinental

Hotel was considered essential to the economy and a limited number of permits were provided to it. Following the arrival of our baby daughter in January of 1968, Shelley and I had moved from the cottage to Paladhy House, the home of Shelley's mother, two brothers, and two of the sisters. The house was located about two kilometres from the hotel, and the permit was needed so I could go to and from work. No fuel was available so no public transport such as taxis, rickshaws, or buses were on the road, and there was, of course, also no petrol for the family cars, so I borrowed a bicycle.

The civil unrest escalated, and business in the hotel plummeted, but the few guests who remained deserved the international quality service the hotel provided, so I needed to continue to attend work on a daily basis. I would do so, taking the same route during daylight hours, riding my bicycle with one hand on the handlebars and one hand holding the permit aloft. It was an unnerving experience. One Sunday morning, curiosity trumped common sense, and I decided to cycle somewhat farther afield in order to see what was happening, a potentially foolish decision. The streets were deserted, and the only sounds I heard were the shouts directed at me from behind closed doors or high walls. Since I didn't understand the language these were possibly suggestions that I return home. Those who might have seen me must have wondered at the strange sight of a young white man riding a bicycle, holding his permit in one hand as he made his way along the streets during a curfew in the midst of serious civil unrest! Soon I encountered an army foot patrol, who, upon checking my permit, allowed me to proceed, but strongly advised by the officer in charge to return home. "Go home, for your own safety. There are violent protesters still running through the streets." I took the advice to heart. Even as the civil unrest gained momentum, the hotel continued to operate, and I continued to ride my bicycle to and from work on a daily basis, all the while feeling that the time for us in this troubled country must surely soon be ending. This feeling of doom increased, as the violence escalated, and from Paladhy House balcony, where one of the main roads leading to the centre of the city was visible, at night we could see roaming gangs throwing petrol bombs, setting cars and buildings alight. Smoke and flames were visible over the city of Dacca, and in the aftermath of each night's terror, we learned of the horrible acts perpetrated against the victims of this mayhem.

Early on the morning of February 4, 1969, I received a call from InterContinental Hotel's corporate office in New York advising me that Fred Peelen has requested I be transferred to open the Nairobi InterContinental Hotel. Asked if I was willing to transfer? My response was immediate: "Absolutely." My heart raced with the excitement of moving to where nature was still it's most majestic, where lions, elephants and rinocereous in their natural habitat still roamed the plains.

It was time to go. My assistant manager was capable of taking over in Dacca. Following a farewell cocktail party and the presentation to us of an engraved silver tray in recognition of our time at the Dacca InterContinental Hotel, by the end of February 1969, Shelley, myself and one-year-old Erika were on our way to my new assignment in Nairobi, Kenya.

Shelley and I on our wedding day in Bangkok

Shelley at the gate of our first home

Chapter Three

A Brief History of the Roy Paladhy Family

All Hindus belong to a gotro, or what might be understood in Western society as a clan. Their origins trace back to their founders for whom they were named. The Roy-Paladhy family is a member of the Brahmin gotro Kashyap, and their lineage begins with the sage Kashyapa.

At the time of Kashyapa, their ancestors were prominent members of the city of Kanauj, near Kanpur, in the present-day State of Utter Pradesh. During the eleventh century AD, the king of Birbhum, Bengal, invited some of the Brahmin families from Kanauj to relocate to Birbhum in order to educate and perform Vedic rites and rituals in his kingdom.

India then was a collection of individual kingdoms ruled by kings and maharajahs. By royal decree, these families were awarded either land or villages, and Maharishi Dhakha, the family's first identifiable ancestor, was gifted the village of Paladhy. As was common at that time, Maharishi Dhakha took the village name as his surname, and the family Paladhy was born.

Little more is known of the Paladhy families until around 1500 AD, when one Shri Roop Chand Paladhy was awarded the title "Roy" by the ruler of the district of Birbhum in recognition for his exemplary work as a collector of taxes, and the family surname became Roy-Paladhy. Roy, which was a title then, has subsequently morphed into a not uncommon family surname in Bengal.

Between then and the 1700s AD, the Roy-Paladhy families began to move out from Birbhum. Shri Ramachandran Roy-Paladhy, along with his immediate family, migrated to the village of Sunagar in the Dhaka District of Bengal. Many generations later, his descendant Bijoy Kumar Roy-Paladhy, Shelley's paternal grandfather, started his work life as a police officer and, in the latter part of his career, became a crisis manager for major landowners.

Her maternal grandfather, Jagandra Bhattachajee, was a surveyor in the tea gardens of Assam, where Shelley's mother, Lila, was born. Shelley's father, Shukumar Roy-Paladhy, was a telephone and wireless engineer with the post and telegraph department in Calcutta (Kolkata), where the family lived during the British rule in India. He held the rank of lieutenant; it was usual for civil servants of a certain level and/or function to hold military officer rank at the time.

Shukumar and Lila had ten children, seven girls and three boys. While one of the boys died at a very young age, the rest of their children have lived or are living normal, healthy, productive lives. Shukumar passed away in 1956, leaving Lila widowed with their ten offspring. Some were teenagers, Shelley was just thirteen, four were younger children, and some were young adults. Dolly, the oldest of the siblings, was newly married, Sunil, second oldest, was studying in university but left in order to work and support the family, and Nellie, the second oldest sister, became 'household manager' in order to assist her mother. Lila was a strong and generous woman, and her caring, ethical, and kind-hearted adult children have lived their lives as a testament to her legacy.

Given the uniqueness of the Roy-Paladhy name and how it evolved, it is unsurprising that while researching the family history, Shelley and I were unable to identify any 'Roy-Paladhy' family outside of Shelley's immediate one. Also, it appears that there are only fifty-two Paladhys in total. Fifty in India are unknown but are surely distantly related to Shelley's immediate family. There are only two Paladhys elsewhere and they're in the USA: Shelley's younger brother Sujit and, by marriage, his wife, Nigar.

Seven of Shelley's siblings

The eighth sibling, Sujit, the youngest

Chapter Four

A Time in Syria

Our journey to Kenya included a stopover in Syria to spend a couple of weeks with friends. We flew from Dacca to Karachi and onward by MEA, Middle East Airlines to Beirut. With no freight to ship, we had only personal luggage to bring onboard: baby's toys, suitcases, several additional pieces of hand luggage, and the small brass table given as a wedding pesent to Shelley, by the children in the school she taught before joining InterContinental Hotels. While there was a lot of it, airlines were more liberal with the weight of baggage in those days.

Following a night at the Karachi InterContinental Hotel, the next morning, we headed for the airport and our flight to Beirut, then referred to as 'The Paris of the East'. Many helping hands from kindly fellow passengers made the transportation of the luggage from terminal to aircraft go smoothly, and as we settled down in our seats, we were excited at the adventure before us.

Maggie and Cyril Halstead, whom we knew from Dacca and now lived in Damascus, Syria, would meet us at the airport in Beirut. When they heard that I was being transferred for the opening of the new Nairobi InterContinental Hotel in Kenya and Shelley and I would pass through the Middle East, they'd invited us to visit them.

The plane landed, the luggage was retrieved, and we made our way through customs and immigration and out into the arrival hall to be greeted by the welcoming smiles of our friends.

"The car's outside. Let's load up the luggage and be on our way," said Cyril.

The drive from Beirut to Damascus was about 120 kilometres and would take a couple of hours, that is, if there was no delay at the Lebanon-Syria border, which might very well be unlikely. Peace in the whole region was still tenuous. While the '67 war between Israel and several Arab states was over, there were no serious diplomatic efforts to resolve their issues. In September 1967, the Arab states formulated the "Three Nos" policy: no peace, no recognition, and no negotiation with Israel. In March 1969, Egyptian President Gamel Abdel Nasser officially declared a "War of Attrition" against Israel, resulting in formalizing the continuing hostilities that had, in fact, really not stopped after the Six Day War and lasted until August 1970, when a ceasefire was finally declared.

We left East Pakistan as civil society began to crumble, with rampant unrest, the burning of buildings and the mayhem of death and destruction, with soldiers on the streets attempting to contain ever-increasing unrest, which, within a couple of years, resulted in a major revolution and the founding of the country of Bangladesh.

Now I wondered if being here in the Middle East, albeit just for a short visit, was such a good idea.

We set off on the road to Damascus, driving out to the east of Beirut, over the southern end of the Lebanon Mountains, through the fertile Bakke Valley and up into the Anti Lebanon Mountains with a dusting of winter snow still on their peaks, towards the Syrian border, where we would hopefully clear Syrian immigration without a problem and receive our visas. During those troubled time in the late sixties, many European countries, particularly the UK and Germany, along with the United States, maintained a pro-Israeli position, and their citizens were not always welcome in Syria.

When we arrived at the border, there were several Europeans

awaiting visas, and I learned that there were also a couple of German journalists who had been there for three days in the hope of being allowed entry. It became very apparent how valuable our Irish passports were when the immigration officer looked at them and stamped them within a matter of minutes: 'Entry Valid Three Months'. Ireland's political position at this time was focused on support for the Palestinian right to a homeland and self-determination.

We were now in Syria and about halfway to our friends home, where we planned to stay for a week to ten days. They had an apartment in a very pleasant residential area on the outskirts of Damascus. From their balcony, one could see the mountains we had crossed on the way from Beirut, and on the opposite side of the street was a large, unidentified, nondescript grey government building.

Hafiz al-Assad was defence minister at this time, and it was the following year in November 1970 that he seized control of the country. Prior to that time, he was in a protracted power struggle with Salah al-Jadid, the army chief and effective leader of Syria since the overthrow of the civilian government in 1966. So, not only was Syria in an external struggle because of it's participation in the "Three Nos" policy, but domestically, governance was considerably less than stable.

On two occasions, Shelley and I witnessed events that demonstrated both these facts. One night, while sitting out on the balcony, enjoying drinks, the evening's tranquillity was suddenly shattered by an ear-pounding roar, quickly melding into a painfully sharp scream. As we looked in the direction of the mountains from where the sound seemed to come, we saw, for just a moment, fast-moving aircraft flying very low as they strafed the mountainside with tracer bullets and rockets. Massive explosions ensued, and as suddenly as it began, it was over, except for the huge white-orange flames that burst open like angry volcanos spewing flaming debris into the air, against the backdrop of the moonless, starless night sky.

The following day, it was reported that an Israeli aircraft had bombed a washing machine factory. The believability that the factory was only manufacturing washing machines was questionable.

The second incident occurred shortly thereafter, when we were in bed one night. It was maybe two or three in the morning when we heard a convoy of military vehicles arrive at the 'nondescript' government building opposite the apartment complex. It was not generally known what this building was for, or what government entities it housed, as there was usually little or no traffic, either vehicular or pedestrian, seen coming or going. On this occasion, however, the many occupants of the vehicles appeared to be military personnel, judging by their attire. From the darkened apartment, Shelley and I watched them stealthily enter the building, and shortly thereafter, they withdrew, got into the jeeps, and just as quickly as they had arrived, departed. While we could not determine if as many exited the building as entered due to the large number of individuals involved, rumours we subsequently heard suggested some high-ranking individual or individuals were no more. Of course, they were rumours, and no public acknowledgement ever supported that theory.

Notwithstanding these incidents, life for the ordinary citizen in Damascus appeared no different than any other city, and we enjoyed our time in Syria. We toured the Souks, walking the streets of "the Old City", with its ancient architectural styles reminiscent of the people who lived there, the Romans, Muslims, Christians, and Jews. We visited, among many other historical places, the Umayyad Mosque, originally built by the Roman emperor Constantinople the First and said to contain the head of John the Baptist. It was like walking back in time. We attended parties and met many of the Halsteads' friends.

Maggie was a confidant to many of the young English women, of which there were quite a few, married to Syrian men. She helped them deal with some of the cultural challenges they faced. Some of these young wives were not entirely happy, and one or two they met abandoned their life in the male-dominated society of Syria and returned to England.

During this time, I was in contact with the InterContinental Hotel in Nairobi, awaiting travel instructions, and shortly before our expected week or ten-day visit to Damascus was due to conclude, I was advised that the hotel was behind schedule and I was not required for a further six weeks. This was an awkward situation as it meant either imposing ourselves on our friends for an extended period or possibly going back to Beirut and staying at the Phoenician Hotel, which was the nearest InterContinental Hotel and the most convenient location for the eventual onward journey to Kenya. Neither Maggie nor Cyril would countenance our departure, and they insisted we remain with them as long as was necessary.

One of the most memorable occasions during our time in Damascus was an invitation from Cyril's local counterpart to his home for dinner and to meet his family. Mr Azrak was an engineer, a quiet man of gentle disposition whose wife was a senior government employee. Their flat was very modest, with a tiny front room that served as a sitting room and dining room, a couple of very small bedrooms, and a galley-size kitchen. Yet the warmth of their welcome, their generosity, and their hospitality, along with the incredible food they provided, were unmatched in my experience either before or since.

They showered Shelley with gifts, including a gold ring, a gold pendant, and a beautiful dress length of gold-thread embroidered brocade. Mrs Azrak even apologised that the brocade was not six metres long to have as a sari. It was both a humbling and somewhat embarrassing experience given that we brought no reciprocal gifts.

Their table was laid with a vast array of mezze, which was followed by a beautifully presented, large baked fish on a silver tray. Believing this to be the main course, we relished the feast. However, it was not, and dishes of lamb and flavoured rice soon appeared, and the sweets that concluded the meal were the sweetest and richest I had ever tasted. As we departed at the conclusion of the evening, our hosts were effusive in their thanks for coming to their home. This was indicative of the warmth of the Syrian people Shelley and I met during our time in Syria.

Within a couple of days of that evening I received instructions advising me that we could now travel to Nairobi. This was accompanied by a set of airline tickets that would bring us from Beirut to Cairo and on to Nairobi.

We packed, rented a taxi and headed back to Beirut. The ride by taxi was very different from when we had first been driven from Beirut to Damascus. Fear did not appear to be an emotion the Syrian taxi driver possessed, and I silently prayed we would make it to Beirut in one piece. My pleas to go slower down the side of the mountain on the winding corkscrew road were ignored, and we made the journey in record time, a record we would have preferred to forego given the state of our nerves.

This wild drive reminded me of a similar experience when I was eighteen. I was hitchiking through France and failing to get a lift on one occasion, I ended up on a dark road having walked for several hours through high hilly countryside. It was raining; the raindrops bouncing hard on the black tar road under a starless night sky. I was soaked and exhausted, so I pitched my tent in a field near the roadside. Following a restless night I arose to a bright dawn, the rain had passed and I set about hitching a ride. Several cars passed, ignoring me. Eventually after about an hour, one young man stopped in what was a 'top of the range' Citroen. He was expensively dressed although flashily so, and his car was new, red, the colour of bright red polished apples. It was shiney, spotless and 'fully loaded'.

"Where are you off to man"? he asked in french accented english.

"Trying to get to Paris" I responded.

" I'll drop you as near as I can, throw your stuff in the boot and hop in"

We drove off, tires screeching, smoke billowing, as the 'G' force pushed me back in my seat, and I wondered, now trapped, if I would survive the craziness. We careened at high speed, down the corscrew road for about an hour, before arriving at a ramp onto the Autoroutes. I exhaled, I could relax again now that we are approaching a straight multilane highway, we must surely be safer. But no, my fear morphed into fearful panic. For as we entered the Autoroutes an oncoming old car driven by a elderly man, changed lanes and slammed into us, pushing us to the side of the road and badly damaging the Citroen's front fender. The beautiful red car body crumpled like a discarded old newspaper. What I concluded must be French expletives, 'seemed to colour the air blue' as my drivers temperature rose and in a fit of rage, he shockingly pulled a handgun from his glove box, with the contents of the weapon intended for the other motorist, the recipient of his anger. He opened the car door, charged over towards the elderly driver, waving the pistol about as he fired off a shot in the air. This was beyond frightening and I had no desire to wait around to learn the consequence of such rage. I quickly opened the car door, jumped out, grabbed my stuff and ran back up the ramp onto the country road to await another lift.

We survived this drive from Damascus, and spent the night at the Phoenician InterContinental. Early the following morning, we set off for the airport and the flight to Cairo. It was a short flight, and in Cairo we had several hours wait before the Nairobi flight. We rented one of the small rooms that were available at the Airport, where we rested and freshened up.

Chapter Five

Nairobi, Kenya

Around midday on April 5, 1969, our second wedding anniversary, Shelley, myself and one-year-old daughter, Erika, along with our mound of personal luggage and the brass table, boarded the East African Airways flight to Nairobi, Kenya, where we expected to spend the next two years, the length of my contract. I thought about the adventure awaiting us and reflected on the whirlwind past three years. In just that short time since I left the family home in Ireland, without ever having lived alone, where my mother cooked my meals and did my laundry, my life had changed. I was now married with a family, had worked in two locations in Asia, experienced the beginning of a revolution in East Pakistan, witnessed the periphery of war in the Middle East, and was now on my way into the continent of Africa. Daunting, yet exciting!

The flight took approximately four hours, and upon landing in Nairobi that evening, we were warmly greeted at the airport by Fred Peelen, the hotel's general manager. Of course, since we worked together in Dacca, we knew each other well. We drove the relatively short distance to the Nairobi InterContinental Hotel, where we would stay until after the hotel opening some six weeks later.

After the lush tropical growth of East Pakistan and the desert of Syria, along the highway from the airport to the city, the wide open space, was lined on both sides by a rolling mixture of vegetation, certainly not the green of the tropics and also not the dust of the desert, but a sort of green-beige hue of partly sunburned grass and scrub. We passed a drive-in cinema en route, and I relished the purchase of a car and the opportunity to watch movies in the open air under a star filled sky on a warm evening, coke and popcorn in hand and Shelley by my side. Much better than the sofa and T.V.!

While the hotel rooms were ready, as yet there were no kitchen facilities installed in the hotel, so all meals necessitated a trip to the New Stanley Hotel, where arrangement had been made to provide the expatriate staff with regular breakfasts, lunches, and dinners. The New Stanley was an old property located on Kenyatta Avenue, the main street, and just a short walk from the InterContinental. It was one of only a couple of hotels in Nairobi, including The Pan Afric, somewhat approaching international standards. The Nairobi InterContinental would be the first truly international hotel in the city, and indeed, in Kenya.

Nairobi, the capital and largest city in this East African country, was a pretty city of half a million souls. It has since grown six or sevenfold to become one of the most important and largest cities in East Africa. Its elevation above sea level is about one and a half thousand meters, so it enjoys a sub-tropical highland climate, with temperatures range between ten degrees and twenty-five degrees centigrade—a beautiful climate that was very much appreciated by us after the heat and humidity of East Pakistan.

Kenya became a republic in 1963, when it gained independence from Britain. Jomo Kenyatta, a political activist at that time, was accused of being involved with the Mau Mau, identified as a terrorist group by the British and freedom fighters by the locals, and he was imprisoned, although there was never any evidence of his involvement with the Mau Mau. He was the first president of the country, a position he still held in 1969, and is considered "father of the nation". He would cut the ribbon that officially opened the InterContinental Hotel Nairobi.

The pre-opening period was hectic, as it had been in Dacca with a very similar set of procedures. I selected about one hundred candidates, and at the second interview, narrowed these down to the final forty that was my budgeted staffing level.

None of the new employees in any of the hotel departments had any experience. Some even needed to learn how to wear shoes and the purpose of knives and forks. And these were going to be waiters, waitresses, and bartenders in the hotel's coffee shop, gourmet restaurants, cocktail bars, and banquet rooms, cooks in the kitchens, front office receptionists, and housekeeping room attendants. It was a daunting task, but there were a substantial contingent of experienced and highly competent expatriate staff, along with the head office opening team, who usually participated in all the hotel openings, there to navigate the process. These two groups numbered about forty in total and would ensure a smooth and successful opening.

It was also necessary for all the new equipment to be commissioned and operating satisfactorily, that operating supplies were in stock, and that staff training plans were completed and ready for implementation. With about six weeks to go and forty staff to train with the help of the regional laundry director, there was hardly time for anything but work, eat, and sleep, and little enough of the latter. The 'third world', as the more currently termed 'developing world' was referred to in the sixties, continued to require the help of Western expertise on it's journey to modernity.

During this pre-opening time, Shelley was left to her own devices. She would stroll in the park near the hotel with Erika, or sit in the unfinished hotel lobby, reading. On one such occasion, while in the lobby, the phone at the front desk rang, and as no staff was around to answer it, Shelley took the initiative and did so. The call was for an associate of Fred Peelen, the general manager, who was with him in the hotel bar just off the lobby, undoubtedly giving one of the new bartenders an opportunity to practice his cocktail mixology. When she approached them regarding the call, she reminded Peelen of her own prior experience as a receptionist in Dacca, and Peelen's retort was,

"I thought you'd never ask. Would you be willing to work at reception? You'd be really helpful."

And so, contrary to common practices in the company that discouraged employment of the spouse of department heads, Shelley was so valued for her warm outgoing personality, her commitment to any task at hand, that the rule was bent—actually, broken would be more accurate.

So, she re-joined the company at the Nairobi InterContinental Hotel as a front-desk receptionist. Consequently, it was necessary to find a nanny to look after Erika. With a recommendation from one of the hotel staff, Jamilla was identified and hired. She was an inexperienced young lady who had to be carefully instructed how to care for a one-year-old, and as she learned, she became quite reliable and, indeed, attached to Erika, who learned to communicate with her in Swahili, the language of much of East Africa.

The hotel opened to much fanfare, with president Jomo Kenyatta cutting the ribbon and touring the property. I showed him around the laundry, explaining some of the tasks that the staff was performing. The following day, the hotel opened its doors to the public and guests, with Shelley at the reception desk and me in the laundry.

It was time for the expatriate staff that had resided in the hotel prior to opening to move out, and to accommodate them, the company had leased a group of small, one-bedroom bungalows located a couple of kilometres from the hotel. This worked for all of the expatriates, who were either couples or singles. Since we were the only expatriates with a child, we were given the option of finding our own accommodations, for which the company would pay the rent and utilities.

We located a furnished apartment over a row of shops near the Pan Afric Hotel, on a hill overlooking the city, a couple of kilometres from the InterContinental Hotel. It was a new development, and the apartment, though small, suited us perfectly. We moved in on a month-to-month lease, which, as it transpired, was fortunate since we vacated the apartment a month later.

Time for me to purchase that much-awaited car, and I succumbed to temptation and bought a convertible MGB. Totally impractical, of course, since I had a wife, a baby, and her nanny. I rationalised that I could probably squeeze Erika, being only a small child, and her nanny, Jamilla, into the tiny back seats of the MGB. But Shelley disagreed, reminding me of the impracticality of this choice. Within a week, the MGB was returned to the dealership, to be replaced by the much more suitable Renault 4, a terrific little car very well suited to the rough off-road terrain of the Kenyan countryside as well as the streets of Nairobi.

One evening following a night out, we returned to the flat and decided to have a coffee before retiring for the night. Approaching the stove, we heard a rustling sound from within, and as I gingerly opened the door, we were startled by two enormous rats scurrying around inside. A quick slam of the oven door, and the decision to move was an immediate consequence. We concluded that the rats must have come from a construction site at the rear of the building. We could not risk a repeat performance with a small child around. The next morning, I informed the real estate agent we rented the flat through, who organised an immediate move to a rather nice bungalow in Westland, which was the premier residential area in Nairobi.

Life settled into a regular routine, and new friendships were formed. Saturday nights frequently consisted of a poker game and dinner at our house. A group of about five or six of the expatriate staff would participate, while any wives or partners who might accompany them would take care of dinner. I was a fairly decent poker player, and frequently, my 'pot' was 'in the black'. It was the fun of the game and the social intercourse that was the purpose, so any winnings helped covered the cost of the food and beverage on those nights.

Sunday was the regular day off, as a six-day workweek was the norm in those days within the hospitality industry. The day was frequently spent visiting a game reserve or an upcountry inn for lunch. Lake Navasha was one favoured destination about an hour's drive from Nairobi, and the thousands of pink flamingos that gathered there was like one great pink blanket that covered the lake, a truly incredible sight. Whenever we were off work we took the opportunity to visit game reserves. It was a true privelige to view the great variety of animals in their natural habitat, lions, elephants, giraffes, monkeys and more.

On another occasion, we decided to drive deep into the rift valley, and while on that trip, we encountered a group of Masai tribesmen. The tribesmen happily posed for photographs, holding spears in one hand and Erika in another. Following this photographic session, I gave them a few packets of cigarettes and the bottles of water brought with us especially for that purpose. The Masai continued to live their lives in the old traditional ways, hunting and living off what they killed, just as they had done for millennia, unlike most of the other tribes in Kenya, who had acquired varying degrees of modernity.

In those days life in Kenya was peaceful and enjoyable, with work a pleasure and friends and family a delight. But that peace was soon shattered! On July 5, 1969, a Saturday afternoon, Tom Mboya, minister for economic planning and development, was gunned down in a hail of bullets on Moi Avenue in Nairobi. He died in an ambulance on the way to the hospital. He was thirty-eight years of age and a bright, up-and-coming popular political star. Many believed he would succeed Kenyatta as president of Kenya. He left a wife and five children. Nahashon Isaac Njenga Njoroge, who was later arrested and subsequently hanged for the murder, said at the time of his arrest, "Why don't you go after the big man," feeding into several conspiracy theories, none of which were ever publicly explored. Who he claimed to be "the big man" was never divulged.

The day of the funeral, the procession made its way to the church, passing directly in front of the InterContinental Hotel. It was a bright sunny day and thousands of Mboya supporters chanting their grief, thronged the streets in front of the hotel, which was located near the church. When President Jomo Kenyatta arrived to attend the funeral, skirmishes broke out, first unnoticed, but as they increased in intensity they soon turned into large-scale riots. The police initially lost control and two people were shot dead, with dozens more injured. Many of the demonstrators believed that Kenyatta was somehow involved in the death of Mboya. As the situation looked ominous, the hotel staff was quickly deployed to emergency security duty. I went to the hotel lobby to assist the doormen and concierge staff secure all entrances. The hotel general manager announced over the loudspeaker system that doors were to be locked, with no one, guest or staff, permitted to leave.

Some tourists refused to be dissuaded and insisted on going outside in spite of the obvious threat to their safety, their curiosity stifling their common sense. As a manager on the spot, I advised them that if the situation deteriorated any further, the hotel management would not endanger guests or staff who remained inside by unlocking doors should there be any possibility of an encroachment by the demonstrators into the hotel. Hundreds of demonstrators began moving toward the hotel doors, pressing up against the lobby windows, moving to and fro in waves, attempting to gain entry. Mob mentality was taking over. Riot police were eventually on the scene, and tear gas helped disperse the crowd. The tear gas was sucked into the hotel lobby area through the air conditioning system, and soon many inside suffered its effects as equally as did the demonstrators. It was a small price to pay for the hotel, guests, and staff to remain unscathed. The guests who'd left earlier, against my advice, returned later that evening, rather sheepishly acknowledging their folly. They had taken shelter and were unhurt except for their pride.

The funeral was over, the crowds dispersed, the clean-up around the hotel grounds was completed, the air-handling units cleared out the tear gas, and business, work, and life returned to normal. As both Shelley and I worked, we would frequently eat out before returning home in the evening, while Jamilla would remain to give Erika her evening meal, sometimes staying overnight if the hour was late. On one such occasion, Shelley discovered that she was missing a gold bangle, and when questioned, Jamilla admitted taking it. She was dismissed, and a new nanny, Maria, was found for Erika. She was a big, portly, jolly woman, a stereotypically African mama.

My contract with the hotel was until April 1971, so I expected to remain in Nairobi for the duration. It was now December 1969, barely nine months into my two-year term. While the company could decide to offer a transfer to another property during the period of a contract, they rarely did so, but that's exactly what happened to me. Bea, the General Manager's secretary, phoned me in my office one December morning. "Colm, Mr. Peelen would like to see you. Can you come to the office?" "Yes sure,". I was unconcerned. There were no issues with my department, and everything was running very smoothly. Shelley was also considered a very valuable asset to the front desk because of her prior experience, having guided much of the local reception staff through the hotel opening and beyond. We were content and enjoying life in Kenya.

"Colm, I've received instructions from New York that concerns you," said Peelen

InterContinental Hotels Corp. was owned by Pan Am Airlines at that time, with the head office located in the Pan Am Building in New York City.

"Max Herr has asked for you in Dublin as laundry manager for the three hotels in Ireland."

I was stunned, speechless. This was not what I desired. I'd left Ireland four years earlier not because circumstances forced me to do so, but because the opportunity of my life's grand adventure presented itself, and I had come to believe life was just that, a grand adventure. I did not want to relinquish that dream by returning to a place that might trap me into an indefinite routine, into the mundane, maybe never again to experience other places and other cultures as I had this past four years. That was not who I was or would allow myself to become.

In my late teenage years I had come to understand my fathers anguish with his work life. I was determined this would not be me. Maybe much of my life was about running away from the ghost of my father's own work life? I was devastated, and would resist. I told Peelen, "I don't want this transfer, can't you help me with corporate on this?"

Peelen understood, and he wanted to keep me in Kenya. He advised head office accordingly, but to no avail. Shortly thereafter, instruction came back that I was expected to accept the transfer, and Fred Peelen's advice to me was to do so gracefully. He suggested the company would not look kindly on me being difficult, and as Max Herr was senior to Fred Peelen, he would win the battle anyway. I had worked for Herr in Dacca. We knew each other and got on well together, so there was no concern regarding the working relationship, and it was a promotion with added responsibility for three properties. So, notwithstanding my disappointment in leaving Nairobi, I accepted the inevitable and began to prepare for the transition. The Renault 4 was advertised and quickly sold. Most of the household items were given to Maria as some small compensation for the loss of her job, and several loaded-down car journeys were made to her house.

Travel arrangements were organized, and some basic winter clothes were purchased; in Kenya, the selection of winter clothing was limited. A farewell party was held in the hotel, with the inevitable presentation of parting gifts. Christmas was celebrated, and on December 28, 1969, exactly three years and eleven months to the day after I'd left my hometown, Shelley, myself and a very sick Erika with a high fever, departed Nairobi on a flight to London, and then it was on to Dublin to face winter, a new job, and whatever this next chapter was to bring.

Shelley and Erika with Masai tribesmen in Kenya

Colm, Shelley, and friend Amparo in Nakuru

Shelley and another friend

Chapter Six

The Return to Dublin, Ireland

My family and I boarded the British Airway flight to London with no small degree of trepidation. Erika, just a couple of weeks shy of her second birthday, was ill with a high fever, and even though the doctor cleared her for travel, we were concerned. She was well wrapped up in a blanket and whatever winter clothes we could find in the shops of Nairobi, in consideration of both her illness and the expectation of the cold weather to come upon arrival in Dublin.

The crew on the seven-hour British Airways flight were magnificent. They could not do enough to assist, from helping us board the plane to assisting with our luggage, including the brass table, and constantly checking to see if Erika was okay or needed anything. She didn't, in fact, as she slept throughout the flight, which was a consequence of her illness and a good thing, a blessed relief for both her and the parents. By the time we arrived in London, Erika had improved somewhat, no doubt helped by the long sleep, so she was able to walk to the connecting Aer Lingus flight to Dublin.

A little over an hour later, the familiar sight of the North County Dublin coast and the green pastures adjacent to the airport came into view as the plane descended toward the runway at Dublin Airport. It was raining, unquestionably cold rain, it was grey, the sun was well hidden behind the dark, ominous, moisture-soaked clouds. After the past four years spent in latitudes closer to the equator, where bright sunshine surrounded us and warm air enveloped us, I was now gripped by a momentary wave of depression, disappointed that my time in the sun had come to an end and hoped that was temporarly so.

The plane landed, luggage was retrieved, and we made our way out into the arrival lounge to be greeted by the smiling faces of my parents. A quick dash to the car, eager to get out of the cold as quickly as possible, and we were off on the one-hour drive to Hazel Avenue, Kilmacud, on the South Side of Dublin. This was not the home that I had left four years earlier. My parents had moved in the interim about one kilometre from their former home in Mount Merrion.

Standing on the soil of Dublin brought back memories of my youth. How my friends and I regularly frequented the Bailey pub and were often in conversation with the well-known Dublin writer Brendan Behan, although sadly, much of the time, his participation was less than coherent. In the commercial ballrooms in the city centre where we went, having graduated from the tennis and rugby clubs, we favoured the company of more earthy young ladies from working-class neighbourhoods. Their short skirts were more provocative, their makeup slightly less subtle and their perfume more evocative. They seemed less constrained by conservative etiquette and were perceived by the boys as sexier in many cases than the 'South Side' set. A sports car and the willingness to drop a girl home after the dance, ensured a little taste of passion in the parked car before parting company.

But this was in my past, while stored in my memory, it was no longer relevant in my life. I was happy, proud of my beautiful wife and my pretty daughter.

After Shelley and I settled in, unpacking, and having something to eat, it was time to rest after the long journey, and we bid our good nights. We remained in my parents' home for about six weeks while searching for a place of our own. Two years earlier, on a visit to Ireland, we purchased a house in Goatstown, Dublin. We had rented out the house, and there was still almost a year before the lease expired; consequently, we would need to find a home to rent. This proved to be a difficult task as apartments were relatively few in Ireland in those days and the majority of house rentals were council allocated social housing. The demand for, and availability of, private homes was extremely limited as the local population generally purchased houses to live in and not for speculative rental.

The immediate priority for the newly arrived family was the purchase of winter clothes, and our first day was spent shopping for winter wardrobes. On the second day, I decided I would go to the InterContinental Hotel in Ballsbridge and report to Max Herr, the general manager. In spite of wearing many of the newly acquired winter clothes, I felt cold and miserable, even more so than on that horrible day when I'd left Ireland almost exactly four years earlier. Upon meeting me, Max Herr could read the misery on my face and, empathizing with me, suggested I take a few days to acclimatize before reporting for work. The suggestion while accepted, failed to lighten the mood as I returned home.

Many of the laundry staff and management team I met when I first joined InterContinental Hotels Corp. in 1966 remained largely the same, and they greeted me warmly my first day on the job.

However, I was saddened to learn of the death of Phil Hughes, only in his thirties. Phil had been instrumental in me joining InterContinental Hotels, and had left the hotel a couple of years before my return to Dublin, as his health had deteriorated.

I remember the occasion when Phil asked if I was interested in joining the company. He was a multi-talented man who wore several hats. He owned a maintenance company that serviced the equipment at St. Mary's laundry in downtown Dublin City where I was manager at the time. He was also chief engineer and laundry manager at the InterContinental Hotel in Ballsbridge, Dublin, and was responsible for the engineering and laundry departments of the Cork and Limerick InterContinental Hotels. As a frequent visitor to St. Mary's laundry, he and I had established a cordial relationship, and on one of these occasions, after I had been at the laundry for about a year, Phil asked me if I might be interested in joining InterContinental Hotels. This was an opportunity to join a premier international company and it was time to leave St. Marys Laundry.

St. Mary's laundry was a business owned by nuns and staffed by so-called 'wayward' young girls, who were kept in residence. In later years, along with sister organisations, it gained notoriety as one of the infamous 'Magdalene Laundries', where harsh and inhumane treatment was purportedly visited upon the girls in residence as punishment for their 'sins', which, for the most part, was becoming pregnant out of wedlock. I never saw any evidence of ill treatment during my time there, although I would have had no knowledge of what transpired after the workday ended. I was surprised, shocked and saddened to learn in later years of the claims of abuse of these young women in the 'Magdalene Laundries' and hoped that the one I managed, was not party to such behaviour. If it was, should I have known somehow? Should I have been more sensitive to the 'ether'? It bothered me!

My first thought was that Phil was leaving the company. *Must be too much to manage along with his own business.*

"Are you leaving?" I asked.

"Oh no, it's not for here," was Phil's response. "The company needs a laundry manager in Jakarta, Indonesia."

That was Ireland in 1965, and nobody emigrated anywhere except to England, and maybe a few to Canada, USA, or Australia. I was unsure if I'd ever read, or heard anything about Jakarta,

Indonesia, and was taken off guard by the question.

"I need a couple of days to think about it."

"Of course," replied Phil. "Perfectly understandable."

Phil called me the next morning. "Colm, there's been a change in the position, and it's for Karachi, West Pakistan, not Indonesia." . Thus my life's great adventure began!

The three laundries in the hotels in Cork, Limerick, and Dublin were well run and had efficient and well-trained staff, so there were no issues to be dealt with. Our lives bowed down to a daily routine, with the potential for boredom and an unchallenging work life born to my imagination. It would grow and loom larger over the next few years, eventually maturing into a decision to make a change in my life.

After much searching, and not a great deal of success in finding the 'ideal home', we eventually had to modify our expectations and accepted a house to rent in Churchtown about six weeks after our arrival in Dublin.

As I was now on home ground, I no longer had any Foreign Service Allowances, so I received no house rental or utility costs from the company, which put some restrictions on what was affordable. The house had three bedrooms and was semi-detached, furnished, and adequately sized. However, it had previously been rented to students and was in a filthy condition. We set about shampooing carpets and soft furnishings, washing walls, cleaning out cupboards, and chopping overgrown weeds in the garden, and moved in after a week of hard labour.

The next essential was the purchase of a car.

Years earlier my first car had been a mini. My maternal grandmother gave me the gift of fifty pounds for a deposit on a nine-month-old Austin Mini. The Mini was an innovative new concept in small cars that was introduced to the market in 1959. Of course, at nineteen when I purchased the car, speed was the need, and I was less cautious with my own car than with my father's which I used to borrow, and disaster soon struck. On a trip to Galway with three friends in the newly acquired Mini, to see The Royal Showband, just outside Mullingar I drove into a bend a little too enthusiastically, spun off the road, and landed in a three-foot ditch. Three days later, we returned to Dublin with the car repaired, the Royal Showband performance missed, and pockets emptied.

Now however, not a mini: a big old car would be cheaper to buy, as the running costs were greater. I bought an old Mercedes 180 for one hundred pounds. It was a bad decision, as confirmed many years later when, at my "This Is Your Life" retirement party in Canada, 'with tongue in cheek', Liam Quinn who was now chief engineer in the Dublin InterContinental, wrote: "Colm being the laundry manager and me only the chief engineer, he had more money than I and owned a Mercedes. Daily after work, he would offer me a lift home as we lived near each other. On many occasions, when his car refused to start he would ask, 'Liam, could you give me a push?' This was a regular event, but each time, with a deadpan poker face, he would ask as though it was a request for the first time."

The old Mercedes 'died' after about six months and was towed away for scrap. A more practical, newer Volkswagen 1600 was purchased, and from then on, driving was trouble free. However, within about six months, a beautiful purple Jaguar Mark 10 with white leather interior and real walnut dashboard and trim was too tempting for me to resist. I sold the Volkswagen and bought the Jaguar.

Two doors down from our house in Churchtown lived the Roaches family. They had a daughter, Ann, who was the same age as Erika, and they became friends, as did the parents of both girls.

Life settled into a routine for the next year: work, play, family, and friends. By then, the lease on the rental house was ending, and we decided to search for a place of our own. We sold the house in Goatstown and purchased an ultra-modern home in "the Laurels",

Terenure, Dublin. It was a small, three-bedroom house with a lot of glass and an open living plan in a gated community—an unusual design for Ireland in those days which appealed to the mostly "yuppie" types who purchased the majority of the approximately forty homes. There was also a small number of retired folks who had "downsized". The houses were not as large or as well constructed as the one we had sold in Goatstown, but the layout of the complex made for a close community, and we made good friends during our time in the Laurels.

About this time my younger brother Declan got married to his Swedish girlfriend. The reception was held following the church service, in an hotel in Blackrock, Co. Dublin for family and friends of the bride and groom. My Jaguar Mark 10 was the wedding car and following the reception, I drove the newly married couple back to our parent's house in Kilmacud, where a small group of the immediate family was gathered to wish the newly wedded couple 'bon voyage' on their married life. More toast were made, the mood was both convivial and celebratory and inhabitions were lowered and tongues loosened. At least mine was!

"Hey Declan, don't you have something more pleasurable to do than hanging around here"? I asked.

I indulged in some further pre-wedding-night banter, all related to activities in the 'bridal suite' and my father took offence. His frowns and disapproving looks were unseen by me as I continued.

"Colm, can you come here a second" he eventually requested as he stood in the doorway of the kitchen. He felt I was indelicate and had embarrassed Declan, I disagreed, told him that he was too serious and an argument ensued between us. The resultant frostiness lasted several weeks, with no communication between us until my mother, acting as peacemaker precipitated the restoration of peace.

By now I had come to recognize two things about my relationship with my father. Firstly, we were not at all alike and viewed the world and life through different coloured lenses, and secondly we have never and would never relate as friends.

Maybe it was generational thing, and I enviously watched T.V. shows or movies that portrayed fathers and sons together on fishing trips, attending football games, or just 'hanging out' together, a relationship I never experienced.

All this negative energy between my father and I, may have begun, and resulted partly from a chilhood memory, that has never left me, and remains as clear and vivid as if it were yesterday.

I but speculate as to it relevance!

I affectionaly remember my maternal grandfather Patrick Barrett. He was a well know 'french polisher' in the city of Dublin during the first half of the twentieth century. He worked on the huge doors of major buildings within the city, such as The General Post Office, The Central Bank of Ireland, and Trinity College among others, and was highly paid for his unique skills. His wife, my grandmother Alice, had her own shop on Parnell Street, so they were financially quite comfortable. My grandfather however, was a 'hail fellow well met' character and was generous to a fault, buying drinks for his pals in the pubs, or giving money to those less fortunate. When I was very young, maybe three or four years old, he bought me my first football. Real leather! We lived right next door to my grandparents in Ballybough, North Dublin City, so I had regular contact with my grandfather. Around that time my grandmother and grandfather seperated for reasons I've never known. He remained in their house and she left, which seemed unusual, at least by todays standards.

After our family went to live in Ballymum, it was maybe a year or so later that I remember the occasion being in the back of my father's Austin Seven as he and my uncle Paul drove to my grandfather's house. They removed their jackets, left them and I in the car and entered the house. I was possibly about five years of age by then and could not say how long I was alone in the car.

76

However, as my father and uncle left the house, rolling down their shirt sleeves upon returning to the car, a unexplained feeling of dread descended upon me. Even as a very young child I shuddered to this feeling of tension in the air and knew something was amiss. Sometime later, maybe weeks or months or longer, I learned my grandfather died in his home by gassing; suspected, possible suicide. I never again saw him after the incident with Paul and my father, and to this day, I don't remember any reference ever again being made of him, by any member of our family.

One of the retired residents of the Laurels, Rose Mosel, with whom Shelley had become quite friendly, was interested in handcraft and invited her to join a group of ladies who met on a regular basis to learn different techniques in hobby crafting. Shelley enthusiastically participated and, after a couple of weeks, produced her first item, a beautiful coffee table with a top of small coloured tiles. It took pride of place in our home. Shelley has continued crafting in various genres ever since, including painting, folk art tole painting, bead making, and greeting card making.

Dan and Winnie O'Shea lived opposite us, and they became friends. Dan was a news editor with RTE, the Irish State TV company, and a fan of a regular glass or two of Guinness. On New Year's Eve, he and Winnie decided to throw a party, and about twenty of their friends and neighbours were invited to what promised to be a real shindig—nothing fancy, but lots of what there was: kegs of Guinness to drink and pigs crubeens (trotters) to eat. Pig's trotters were a hearty, cheap delicacy that complimented the Guinness. They were favoured in Ireland years before the days of the 'Celtic Tiger' and the wealth that it brought, which nourished a more sophisticated Irish palate. Ten pounds in cash was dispatched to purchase the cooked pig's trotters, with the expectation of receiving maybe three or four dozen. However, the delivery van arrived with several large sacks that contained approximately ten dozen of the tender delicacies. Dan had forgotten how inexpensive they were, and appetites at the party were more than satisfied. Analogous to the story of the loaves and fish in the Bible, there were baskets of leftover trotters, so the next day, anyone in the estate who fancied pigs feet for lunch, dinner, or supper were welcome to avail of them. They just had to turn up at the house with an empty container.

Yvonne and Sean lived two doors down from us. Sean was a professional musician belonging to a very popular showband in Ireland at the time, and he earned a very good income. Colour TV had just arrived in Ireland, and it was a very expensive novelty that few could afford, but Sean purchased a set. Some of the neighbours, including us, were invited one evening to see colour TV for the first time. The pictures were grainy, the colours unrealistic, but what was to become ordinary in the coming years was actually quite thrilling that night.

Two years had passed since we returned to Dublin from Nairobi, and the fear of routine and boredom again began to loom large, so I decided to seek a transfer. Before I had an opportunity to approach Max Herr with this request, he called me to his office.

"Colm, I've received instruction from corporate in New York to ask you to transfer."

Without even knowing to where, I was excited at the prospect of a new adventure. It was as if the human resources folks in headquarters had read my mind. I interrupted before he could finish.

"Where to?" I eagerly inquired.

" Abidjan, Ivory Coast."

"Great, when do I report?"

An immediate response, no questions asked,. no answers needed, any conditions were acceptable. This of course, was typical of my impatient nature.

" June; but first, you'll need to do a crash course in French. We'll send you to Alliance Francais."

While I didn't realise it at the time, the fact that I had already been requested by Fred Peelen for Nairobi and Max Herr for the Irish hotels enhanced my reputation at the corporate office and would have been a factor in transferring me back to Africa. The prospects of the upcoming transfer motivated me to study diligently during the French classes. Although I had taken French language classes in school, I'd found them difficult, had not really managed to keep up with the rest of the class and dropped the course after two years.

About halfway through this course, everything changed. One day in early April, I received a call from Max Herr.

"Colm, I have new instructions from New York. The InterContinental Hotel in Hamburg, Germany, has big problems, and they want you to go there instead. They need you urgently so Abidjan is out".

At that time it mattered little to me where I went as long as I went; I was evolving into a country hoping minor adventure junkie. I unhesitatingly agreed. A departure date was set for early May, and at the end of that day, I returned home to tell Shelley that they were not going to West Africa but to Germany.

So we were preparing to move again. We would rent out our house in the Laurels, sell or give away the furniture, and sell the new Mini. Needing the car until our departure date, I would eventually leave it with my father to sell.

Packing was completed, tickets were purchased, and on the day of departure in May 1972, my parents drove us to the airport to catch our flight to London and the onward connection to Hamburg, Germany. We didn't speak German, and unlike the original transfer instructions to Abidjan, when I had taken French classes, no such opportunity for German lessons were available given the urgency of the move.

We bid farewell and boarded the flight, once more on a grand adventure, a little over two years following our arrival in Dublin.

Colm and Shelley in Dublin with the old Mercedes in the
background and brother Declan on the left.

Chapter Seven

Hamburg, Germany, and Cornell University, USA

We had no expectation of being met by anyone from the InterContinental Hotel upon our arrival in Hamburg Airport, and we weren't. My transfer from Dublin to Hamburg did not restore my expatriate status, Germany being within Europe, and as such, it did not warrant the consideration I would have received if I'd transferred to Abidjan, as originally planned, or indeed, to any other developing country that required expatriate management or technical support. There was no one to receive us, no one to help with the search for accommodation, and no foreign service allowance. It was a decent salary for the position, but for the rest, it was like Dublin.

We collected the luggage, cleared customs and immigration, and approached the hotel desk in the arrival terminal in search of accommodations for the following few days. Reservations were made in a small 'pension' within walking distance of the InterContinental Hotel in the centre of the city.

I decided to wait a day or two before reporting for work so we could explore the city centre. After breakfast on the morning following our arrival, we put Erika in her stroller and set off, intending to spend the day exploring the city that was to be our new home. It was a beautiful May morning, the sun was shining, the blue sky was cloudless, and we felt exhilarated.

The Free and Hanseatic City of Hamburg, to give it its full title, opened up before us in all it's historical architectu;ral beauty, as we began our walk. One of Europe's richest cities, dating back to the Holy Roman Empire. A city of magnificent church steeples and flowing canals. It is Germany's second largest city with a population of approximately two million people and a total metropolitan population around five million. Its centre surrounds both the Binnenalster (Inner Alster) and Aussenalster (Outer Alster), the two lakes which were originally formed by damming the river Alster.

We had a city map we'd picked up at the airport information desk, so had a point of reference with the small pension where we were staying. Not able to speak a single word of German, of course, would be a challenge should we require directions. However, as long as we continued to maintain points of reference throughout the walk, we would be fine. It was a new and exciting adventure, and we looked forward to that day and what was to come.

Leaving the pension, and following the map, we walked to the lake, which took about thirty minutes. Eventually, arriving at the park surrounding the Outer Alster. We passed the InterContinental Hotel, where I would begin my new assignment in a day or two. We walked through the park, around the lake to the north side, and continued on until we came to the Inner Alster and the city centre. We stopped for lunch at a large restaurant overlooking the lake and the many tour boats, where we had bratwurst and sauerkraut. After lunch, we continued to walk around the Inner Alster. By late afternoon, we completed a full circle, probably measuring about ten kilometres, and arrived back at the pension. The wonderfully satisfying day was followed by an early evening meal, and we turned in for the night, tired but content.

After breakfast the following morning, I walked to the Hamburg InterContinental Hotel, which overlooked the Alster lake, to report to the General Manager Herr Stangel.

"Welcome to Hamburg, Colm. Good to meet you, hope you journey was okay"?

"Happy to be here Mr Stange and the journey was fine thanks."

"Did you come on your own?"

"No, my wife and daughter are with me.

"Where are they" he asked.

We're in a small pension a couple of kilometres from here."

"What I'd like to do Colm, is to send you in our hotel van to collect your family along with your luggage, and take you to the staff house, where we have a couple of rooms ready for your arrival. The Hausmeister is aware you're coming, so I'll phone him to say you're on the way, and he will meet you when you get there. The rooms are small, but you can probably manage until you decide how and where you would like to live. Give yourself time to get to know the city. Take a couple of days to settle in, and if you come to work at ten am on Monday to the weekly department head meeting, I'll introduce you to the management team and get you settled into your department."

The day was Thursday! With that the meeting ended, I was introduced to the hotel driver, and we set out to collect my family and drive to Schnelsen, a suburb of Hamburg where the staff house was located. It was a large building, four storeys high and containing several hundred small rooms, each consisting of two single bunk beds, a small dining table, two chairs, a small double-sided wardrobe, a washbasin, and a tiny balcony. There was a staff lounge with a TV, a communal kitchen, and a communal shower/toilet facility on each floor.

Many of the hotels and, indeed, other businesses in Germany used 'gest arbeiters', guest workers who usually came from Turkey,

Palestine, and other parts of the Middle East on contract and were provided with accommodation. This was a factor of Germany's booming economy, where the local market could not satisfy the demand for hourly rated employees and housing costs were beyond the means of most 'gest arbeiters'. I was the only member of the management staff who was not German.

We explored the area where the staff house was located, mainly with a view to locating shops and public transport as I was expected into work the following Monday morning. With assistance from the Hausmeister and our own walkabout, we located a grocery shop nearby and the AKN train stop a short distance away, which would connect to the S-Bahn, leaving me at Dammtor Station, just a short walk to the InterContinental Hotel.

As this was not an expatriate posting with a fixed term, I was on an open ended assignment, so we could be living in Hamburg for an indefinite period, and it was important to feel comfortable with the country, the city, and the lifestyle.

Monday morning at eight am, on May 15, 1972, I set off for the first day of my new assignment. The hotel is in one of the most beautiful locations in this beautiful city. It overlooks the park and the Alster, and it has about 350 guest rooms and a variety of restaurants, bars, and banquet facilities. Some forty years later, I learned that the hotel was to be demolished and a newer, grander InterContinental Hotel built in its place.

On the following Monday, I was introduced to the management team and participated in the weekly department head meeting. Language was not a problem at this stage, as all of the management team spoke fluent English, but it would become so later, requiring me to eventually attend German language classes at the Berlitz School.

The person I would work most closely with was the executive housekeeper, an elegant lady with a long history in the hospitality industry and just a few years from retirement. She expressed her great relief that I was there, commenting,

"Herr Madden, you have many challenges ahead."

The laundry manager whom I was replacing was also in attendance. He had been offered the position of assistant manager but had declined, much to my relief, for why would I want someone to work as my deputy who had, as the executive housekeeper suggested, created "many challenges".

The meeting concluded, and as the executive housekeeper and I walked toward the laundry, she said,

"Just so you know, I've already used up my linen budget for the year because I've not been getting clean linens from the laundry and have had to continuously purchase new stocks, so don't be surprised with what you see."

As we entered the laundry, I was stunned by the scene that unfolded before me. It was total chaos, with restaurant linens and guest room linens up to the ceiling, virtual mountains. Thousands of sheets, towels, pillowcases, tablecloths, napkins were piled up in the used linen bays. Some had obviously been lying there for weeks when they should have been processed daily. The untrained staff were muddling through, oblivious to any system or procedure. *No wonder the transfer was urgent.* I immediately set about developing a retraining plan for staff and the implementation of proper systems and procedures, and within a month, the backlog was cleared and the regular service was restored.

With the situation at work now normalised, it was time to look for a home, as four weeks in the cramped staff quarters was becoming untenable. Before leaving Dublin, friends of ours gave us the name and contact details of their friends Shaukat and Inge Chaudry who lived in Hamburg,. They suggested I call them, as they would be only too willing to help with the familiarization of the city. Maybe Inge and Shaukat could help us with the search for a home, so I phoned them one Friday evening and introduced myself and Shelley. Inge answered the phone, was delighted to receive the call, and invited us to visit at their home in Norderstedt on Sunday afternoon for 'Kafe and Kuchen', a German tradition. Inge provided directions on how to get there, and on Sunday, we set off on our first journey through the city by public transport.

The Chaudrys had two children, a son and a daughter, both older than Erika by six or seven years. We enjoyed the afternoon, and both Inge and Shaukat assured us that they would be only too happy to help find a home to rent. This would prove a greater challenge than anticipated, for many property owners were unwilling to rent to a family with children, or in our case, even one child. Eventually, we located a flat which was the converted upper floor of a detached two-storey house. This home was in Schnelsen, directly opposite a large hospital. The flat was small but comfortable, two bedrooms, a living come dining room, a bathroom, and a tiny kitchen.

I purchased a second-hand Volkswagen Beetle so we were mobile. Frau Zwingmann the owner of the flat, persuaded the hospital kindergarten to take Erika, though it was solely intended for the children of staff. Shelley was hired by the InterContinental Hotel as a restaurant cashier and was soon promoted to general hotel cashier. Another breach in company protocol, but we were valued employees.

Shortly into the new year of 1973, a new general manager was appointed for the Hamburg InterContinental Hotel. It was Fred Peelen. A familiar face and good news for me. I'd worked with Peelen in Dacca and had been requested by him for the opening of the Nairobi InterContinental Hotel, and now here he was, my boss for the third time. Fred Peelen regarded me highly, as evidenced by his Nairobi request. I felt confident that I was now being presented with an opportunity to improve my career prospects and that Peelen would help. I would wait until he was settled into the property, before soliciting his support.

In April, approximately two months after Peelen's arrival, I raised the subject of career advancement with him. Within the company there existed divisional positions of 'laundry directors', but with six or seven divisions in InterContinental Hotels Corp., the likelihood of one being available was not great. However, I would ask that it be considered. I would happily leave the laundry if I could get the training and development needed to go into hotel operations, where many more career opportunities would open up. In our meeting, Peelen was enthusiastic and assured me that he was willing to support me in furthering my career. He would begin by recommending me for a divisional laundry director position, and the response from the Corporate Office would determine the viability of that route.

It was not long before this road quickly terminated. There were incumbents in all the four divisions, The Americas, Middle East-Africa, Asia-Australisa, and European Division, and none were leaving anytime soon. So it would be the tougher but potentially more rewarding road that I would embark upon: executive development trainee!

Fred Peelen initiated the process with the corporate human resources vice president in New York in May 1973, outlining a development plan we had jointly felt appropriate. He requested that I be appointed to the Corporate Executive Development Program, of which two candidates were selected from each division annually. Unfortunately, the response was negative. While corporate would look very favourably on my career post any training because of my obvious management abilities, I was not a hotel school graduate and had no operational experience outside of the laundry, so they felt they could not set such a precedent. It was a bitter disappointment. However, encouraged by the affirmation that I was viewed favourably in HQ, Fred Peelen was willing to mirror the corporate program at the Hamburg Hotel.

I decided I had to take this opportunity if I was to have a more progressive career. There would be sacrifices, and I would have to discuss these with Shelley, for they would not only be mine alone, but also hers, so her participation in the decision was essential. Shelley's response to the proposal was immediate and completely supportive.

"Colm, if you believe in this, then let's do it. We'll make it work, we'll do whatever's needed."

And so, the wheels were put in motion.

The program would take two years, with six summer weeks in each of those years at Cornell University – School of Hotel Administration in Ithaca, New York. The rest of the time would be at the Hotel in Hamburg.

The School of Hotel Administration at Cornell University was founded in 1922. is renowned and considered the best in the world. The hotel in Hamburg had not budgeted for such a program and so could not fund it entirely. I would take a fifty percent drop in salary, forgo my annual management bonus, and fund the Cornell University courses myself. It was a huge financial commitment, and we were left with no option but to sell the house in the Laurels in Dublin.

It was not long before a deal was done, contracts were signed, the mortgage was paid off, and the equity cash was lodged in our bank account. Also, we could no longer afford the Hamburg apartment, and to live as a family in the staff quarters for almost two years was not a viable option.

We decided that Shelley and Erika would go to Dublin to live with my parents and I would move into the staff house in Schnelsen.

In June, the packing completed, Shelley and Erika left Hamburg for Dublin via Switzerland. They travelled by train to Geneva, to visit friends for a week before flying on to Dublin. Shortly after my wife and daughter's departure, I boarded a Lufthansa Flight to Kennedy Airport, New York, transferred to LaGuardia Airport for a connecting Allegheny flight to Ithaca, New York, and Cornell

University for the first of my two summer sessions.

Cornell is an American Ivy League University, founded in 1865. It is broadly organised into seven undergraduate colleges and seven graduate divisions at its Ithaca campus. The campus overlooks the town of Ithaca and Cayuga Lake, and covers about 750 acres with about 260 university buildings. Cornell counts more than 245,000 living alumni, thirty-one Marshall Scholars, twenty-eight Rhodes Scholars, and forty-one Nobel Laureates affiliated with the university.

The Statler Hotel is owned by the University and is located on campus. It is a full-service luxury property which is an addendum to the hotel school and used for student projects and training.

Based on my experience on the flight to Ithaca, I was unsurprised when, several years later, the Alleghany Airline ceased to exist and was later reinvented as USAir. It was a miserable flight in a 'rattletrap' small turboprop airplane that dripped water onto my head throughout the journey. It might have been condensation, but based on the condition of the aircraft, I suspected it very well might also have been a leaking fuselage.

Upon landing at Ithaca Airport, I took a taxi to the university, and upon arrival and registration, was assigned to my room, No. 109 in Statler Hall, one of the student accommodation houses. I received a familiarization packet that included details of the university and its facilities, information on College Town and the town of Ithaca, along with details of the orientation program scheduled for the following day. The first Monday on campus was orientation, a discourse on the university followed by explanations of lecture halls, dorms, refectories, and other facilities on campus, including a number of restaurants and bars. Classes would start the following day.

My first summer in the hotel school would focus on accounting, starting with basic accounting and progressing to the specifics of hotel financial management. This was the foundation for my two-year executive development program, as a solid understanding of this topic was essential for good business management. I would finish that first summer with a course on front office operation, the process of guest room management and utilization. I felt privileged to be here in the world's most renowned hotel school, with students from every corner of the globe. There were about thirty hospitality professionals in my class, some from as far away as Australia, Mexico, and Germany. Others were, of course, from the United States, as well as from several other countries. It was a terrific forum for cross-fertilization of ideas from many backgrounds, cultures, and locations. That in itself was of immense value, greatly contributing to the overall learning process.

As the introductions were made in class and people settled into the course routine, friendships and alliances developed. I gravitated towards a young married couple, Bob and Terri, who owned a Holiday Inn in Tennessee and had driven from there to Ithaca in their Ford Thunderbird. Both Bob and Terri worked in their property. and both were in Cornell for the whole of that summer. taking the same courses as myself. I also became friendly with two young men, Glenn from Australia. and Jan from Munich, Germany. The courses were intense, and most nights after class, required project work and study groups. Bob and Terri, and Glenn, Jan and I did much of this work together or with one or more of the five of us. None of the group liked to eat in the refectories but preferred to have our meals in one of the restaurants in College Town. These targeted the student body and were inexpensive and served better food than the refectories.

July the Fourth, American Independence Day and a major holiday, was on a Wednesday in 1973, so classes were also suspended for the Monday and Tuesday, the second and third. Bob and Terri took advantage of the long weekend and drove back to Tennessee. Glenn, Jan and I decided we would visit Niagara Falls on a two-day trip, so on the Sunday before the holiday, we took a bus to Canada. Buffalo is the larger city on the American side, and Niagara is the smaller one on the Canadian side. The falls, however, are best enjoyed from Niagara, and also, the *Maid of the Mist*, the tour boat, which goes under the falls, leaves from Niagara.

The bus journey from Ithaca took several hours, and after a further hour's delay at the very busy border crossing, we eventually arrived at the hotel in the late afternoon. That evening was spent strolling along the riverfront, with its profusion of bars, restaurants, and amusements parlours lit up like a mini Las Vegas. We found a place to eat and drink and afterwards enjoyed the spectacular array of ever-changing coloured lighting projected onto the foaming waters as they tumbled over the Horseshoe Falls.

Next morning, bedecked in waterproof coats, hats, and overpants, we boarded the *Maid of the Mist* for a trip under the falls, a forty-minute ride, a fair amount of turbulence, and under the falls, a lot of spray, but a lot of fun. After lunch, we boarded the bus for the return journey to Ithaca, and Cornell.

The courses continued for the rest of the summer, often with an intensity that kept us away from our beds long past midnight. At the end of August, with the successful completion of my courses, diplomas in hand, and newly felt confidence in my ability to translate what I had learned into action back on the job in Hamburg, I headed for New York City and the InterContinental Hotels corporate office on the sixty-seventh floor of the Pan Am Building for my appointment with Jim Hynes, corporate vice president of human resources. Hynes expressed his admiration for what I was doing and assured me that even though they were unable to formally include me as a corporate executive trainee, the company would be very supportive of my training in Hamburg, with its successful conclusion promising a bright future.

Then it was on to Dublin for a short holiday with Shelley and Erika before returning to Hamburg to begin the executive training program. Shelley and Erika were settled into their flat in the upstairs of my parents house and Erika had been admitted to Mount Anvil School.

Back Hamburg InterContinental Hotel, I would spend the next nine months in the departments of food and beverage cost control, purchasing, cashiering, night auditor, income auditor, receivables, payables, and finally as assistant chief accountant. This provided a solid foundation in the discipline of financial hotel management. As it was before the age of computers, manually managed was the method, pen, paper, and mechanical calculator! I would also seek every opportunity during my off time, to learn about areas in which I had not as yet been assigned too. In the evenings I worked in banqueting, giving me exposure to food service, particularly the fast-paced, precisely timed 'silver service' that presented professionally delivered, hot food for up to a thousand guests at exactly the same time, each time, for each course of every meal.

While eager to gain the most from the time I would spend on my development, I did allow myself some personal time. On Sunday, my one day off, I lunched in a small very comfortable "kneipe" or bar opposite the staff house, and always selected the same menu item because it was so good. A glass of fresh, ice-cold draft beer, which took about five minutes to prepare in typical German style, creating a nice, frothy finished 'head', followed by a wonderful wiener schnitzel and brat kartoffel washed down by the second beer.

With so much time spent in the evenings in banqueting and the varying dates on which functions were held, it became difficult for me to regularly attend German language classes at the Berlitz School. It was important to continue learning the language in order to broaden work opportunities, so I sought other options to study.

On one occasion, this subject came up in conversation in the human resources department when the HR administrator, Anna Schutt, suggested that she would be willing to help me with language studies. We agreed that I would go to her apartment two evenings a week for two hours when there were no banquets, so these evening would vary. And so the classes began. While the first few evenings in Anna's apartment were indictive of what one might expect, seating around her dining table with lighting turn up, text books spread out, notes to be taken, and grammer explained, several evenings later was an awkward surprise. As I entered the apartment large cushions were spread out on her living room floor, lights were dimmed and I was greeted with "Hi Colm, I thought we'd start practicing some conversation tonight" The content of the conversational practice began to move in a direction more intimate than I wished and I began to feel uncomfortable. I made some excuse to leave quickly. It soon became apparent that Anna was more interested in me rather than my ability to learn the language, so the classes ended abruptly. This was now an uncomfortable and awkward relationship as she worked in the human resources department, from where much of my training program was administered. She was an attractive girl, she knew I was married and I wondered why she would set her sights on me. Maybe she thought since my wife was living away from me, I might be willing to satisfy some carnal fantasy she may have nutured.

I wasn't!

June of 1974, I again returned for my second summer at Cornell University Hotel School. I had now completed one year of training and had received a solid foundation in food and beverage operations and hotel financial management. The second part of the program focused on rooms management, property operations management, plant management, and marketing. The journey to Ithaca was uneventful, as, indeed, was summer on campus. My studies continued as intensely as before, and while I made friends, because I was taking a variety of courses, they weren't as close as those from the previous summer.

The Fourth of July was a Thursday, and classes were cancelled until the following Monday. I went to New York City for the holiday weekend. I stayed in a small hotel in Manhattan, walked the city streets, including Time Square, went up to the top of the Empire State Building, ate in some great restaurants, and returned to Ithaca on the Sunday.

Early September, having completed my studies, I left Cornell Hotel School for the final time. I spent a week in Dublin with Shelley and Erika before returning to Hamburg.

Back at the InterContinental Hotel in Hamburg, I continued my training, working in the front office, which managed the room inventory and handled reservations, guest check in and check out, room cashiering, and general assistance with guests of the hotel. This was the most challenging part of the whole program for me, as I was continually interacting directly with guests, and it tested my German language skill to its limit. While I managed communications reasonably well most of the time, there were more than a few occasions where I struggled with more complex situations, causing me no small degree of stress. However, I successfully completed training in that department by December 20, 1974, at which time I planned to travel to Dublin for the Christmas holidays.

On the scheduled day of departure, I headed to the airport, and as I approached the desk to check in, there were many passengers ahead of me embroiled in a considerable amount of commotion, with lots of waving hands and arms, along with the din of angry raised voices. I soon learned what all the commotion was about. The airline had that very morning ceased operations, and all their planes were grounded. My flight to London was now cancelled. Approaching the desk and demanding a suggestion for an alternative route to Dublin or, at the very least, the cost of my fare refunded, I failed to get any satisfaction. The response from the staff was;

"Sorry, we can't assist any further, and what you need to do is contact the office in the City Centre after the holidays."

It was a scripted response, and no further comment or assistance would be forthcoming. Since the staff were probably about to lose their jobs, their interest in being helpful had unquestionably waned.

It was a Thursday, and the office was closed until Wednesday, December 26, when they would open only to deal with passengers' claims. Since the airline now appeared to be defunct, no amount of fist shaking, arm waving, or voice raising was going to help or change anything. The only thing to do, if I was to get to Dublin in time for Christmas, was to check if any alternative flight were available. Failing that, I could go back into the city centre to the train station to see if there was an option by land and sea. This was how, I eventually traveled: by train to Le Havre, where I boarded a ferry to Rosslare, and from there, a train to Dublin. Notwithstanding the frustrating and tiring journey, I arrived in Dublin in time for Christmas celebrations. Following the brief holiday, it was back to the Hamburg InterContinental Hotel for the final time to complete my training in engineering and property operations while awaiting a decision from corporate regarding my future.

In mid-March 1975, one morning while I was working with the chief engineer, I received a call from Fred Peelen's secretary.

Peelen broadly smiled as I arrived at his office.

"Come in Colm. I've got great news for you,".

I began to hope this was the opportunity I'd been waiting for. Peelen continued,

"I'm very happy to tell you I've received an offer from corporate for you. You're being offered the position of cost controller for the soon-to-be-opened InterContinental Hotel London. Appointment letter with all the details will be forthcoming soon."

"Oh my God! That's fantastic, I can hardly believe it. Thank you so much Mr. Peelen for everything you've done for me".

I was beyond delighted I was absolutely thrilled. This was an important mid-management job and truly the most beneficial area from which to begin my new career in general hospitality management. I left Peelen's office on cloud nine, with his agreement that I could depart Hamburg any time I was ready and the suggestion that I should take a break before reporting to London in April. On the phone to Shelley in Dublin I babbled out the news. All I had in Hamburg were my clothes, so I packed my suitcase, booked my flight, and left Hamburg on March 21, 1975.

Executive Christmas party in Hamburg InterContinental

Herr Stangel, Shelley, and I at executive Christmas party

Shelley and Colm in Hamburg InterContinental Hotel

Chapter Eight

London, a New Career

My arrival in Dublin Airport was greeted by the broad, smiling faces of Shelley and Erika. We boarded the airport coach destined for my parents' house in South County Dublin, where we would spend a few days before leaving for England. My parents, however, agreed to have Erika remain with them until Shelley and I were properly settled in a home in London.

InterContinental Hotel London was the 'flagship' of the company. It is a five-star, five-hundred-room property located on the exclusive Park Lane and opening in April 1975.

As cost controller, my responsibility was to manage storage, control consumption, and account for and analyse usage of all food, beverage, and general supplies in the hotel's bars, restaurants, banquet areas, and rooms division. I would report to the financial director and have a staff of six, the smallest staff I've ever had in my career. It was a big responsibility, but an exciting and positive beginning to my new career.

This was my third hotel opening, but the first and most important in my new role of 'hotelier'. Consequently, it was much more exciting for me than earlier openings, more intense, more varied, with a greater range of responsibilities, all under the watchful gaze of corporate, since this was one of InterContinental Hotels most important properties. All eyes were focused on a successful opening and ongoing future.

As well as the appointment of a general manager, given the importance of the property, a managing director was also hired as advisor to the management team. He was the renowned French hotelier Max Blouet. He was well known and regarded internationally as the former general manager of the famous George V. Hotel in Paris for over thirty years, and his appointment increased the profile of the London InterContinental Hotel immeasurably. Eventually, he would take me under his wing, and I learned a great deal from him during my time in London. Max Blouet and I would attend wine auctions at Sotheby's to bid for rare vintages. Blouet would guide me through the wine tasting process, helping me understand and appreciate the variety of wines we purchased for the hotel's exclusive restaurants.

Shelley and I arrived at Heathrow Airport, took a taxi to the hotel on Park Lane, met and introduced ourselves to the general manager. We would reside in the hotel during the pre-opening period for approximately six weeks. Shortly after our arrival, while I set up the cost control department, Shelley was offered a position as assistant to the executive housekeeper, which she accepted. This was the third breach of company protocol and a rare occurrence. The extra income would, of course, prove helpful since our financial assets were now depleted following the two years of my training.

The hotel opened, and shortly thereafter, it was time to search for a home. Eventually, we found a flat in the upper part of a private house in Park Royal, near Ealing, one somewhat reminiscent of our accommodations earlier in Hamburg. Shortly after we moved into the flat, my parents flew to London with Erika and stayed about a week before returning home to Dublin.

Erika was accepted into a school a short distance from home and started in September of 1975. She settled in well and usually went off to class in the morning quite happy and cheerful. One evening, however, at dinner, she asked;

"Mummy, what's a solicitor?"

Shelley explained the role in simple terms, saying,;

"If someone did something wrong to you, you could go to a solicitor for advice on what to do about it."

"Mummy, I need a solicitor."

"Why?".

"A boy in school kicked me today, so I need a solicitor."

Both Shelley and I had difficulty concealing our amusement at this whole conversation, and both strained to keep a straight face. Obviously, the kick was not a major incident as Erika was unhurt. "Erika, I don't think you really need a solicitor. You just have to stand up for yourself," Shelley advised.

A few days later, when they were having the evening meal, Erika excitedly piped up;

"I did it, Mummy."

"What did you do?" Shelley asked.

"Got back at the boy who kicked me."

"How?".

"In swimming class today, I got his head and held it under the water."

"Oh, no Erika, you shouldn't have done that it's dangerous. He could have drowned." was the panicked response.

She was seven years old, and the lengthy conversation that immediately followed, explained the principles of appropriate and measured responses, of course, all in language suitable to her age and designed to ensure that never again would such drastic steps be considered. The boy was not hurt, and the school was advised that suitable measures had been taken to communicate to Erika how serious the incident could have been.

Life settled into a regular routine, with Shelley leaving for work daily at six am and I leaving Erika to school at eight and then continuing on to work. Shelley would finish her shift and return home to meet Erika coming from school about three pm, so the timing of work, school and home fitted nicely. Because we both worked and had a young daughter to look after, we had little time for social activities. However, we enjoyed Indian classical music, a musical genre I had come to appreciate from my time on the 'subcontinent'. The renowned maestro of the sitar Ravi Shankar was in concert at the Albert Hall, and we treated ourselves to a rare but memorable musical night out.

My work was progressing very well, and I continued to be highly regarded. The time I spent at the London InterContinental Hotel was one of the most important chapters in my work life, yet also one of the shortest, and it served to expose one of my great weaknesses, my impatience. My desire and expectation to progress to the next level in my career and my unwillingness to bide my time led me to an unwise decision and ended my career with InterContinental Hotels. Within a year of the hotel opening, I resigned from my position and from the company. The general manager and Max Blouet expressed great surprise and disappointment, and my immediate boss, the financial director, told me he was very sad to see me leave.

I was tempted away from InterContinental by the offer of the position of manager of the Great Southern Hotel, Kenmare, Co Kerry, in Ireland, back to my homeland. The consequence of this decision would prove to be considerably more complex and convoluted than I ever could have anticipated. The home in London was packed up, the travel arrangements made, and in early May 1976, we departed London for Dublin and the onward journey to Co Kerry.

Chapter Nine

An Hotelier in Ireland

Early in 1975, I was interviewed for the position of hotel manager for the Great Southern Hotel, Kenmare, Co Kerry. Coras Iompair Eireann (CIE) was the state-owned and operated public transport company of Ireland at the time. It also owned and managed the Great Southern Hotel chain, which had a long and distinguished history with its first two hotels, the Galway Great Southern, dating from 1845, and the Killarney Great Southern from 1854.

The railway companies enjoyed early success at the hight of rail travel, and these two hotels were originally designed to cater to rail travellers, hence their location close to the famous Lakes of Killarney and to Galway Bay, both places immortalised in song and poetry in the tradition of Irish literary and musical culture. From the middle of the nineteenth century onwards, the railway companies not only built railway lines, but also top-quality hotels in resort destinations such as Galway and Killarney, along with others locations. These quality hotels would provide a tourist destination and this would, in turn, promote greater use of train services. Eventually, the Irish state acquired these hotels as part of its acquisition of private railway companies, and their amalgamation formed CIE, the sole provider of all public transport in Ireland. By the 1960s, the growth in the use of cars, motor-inns such as the Torc in Killarney, Rosslare Hotel, and the Corrib in

Galway were added to the company's inventory.

On our arrival in Dublin, we spent a few days in Stillorgan with my parents while I organised the purchase of a car, a two-year-old Ford Cortina. We packed the newly acquired vehicle with our belongings and headed off to Kenmare. Following a five-hour drive, we arrived at our destination and introduced ourselves to the property and its staff.

I had not seen the hotel prior to taking up this appointment, and it was a pleasing introduction. The property was one of the smaller ones in the Great Southern Hotel chain. It resembled a large country house set in substantial gardens. It had sixty bedrooms, a lounge bar, a restaurant, and a small conference room. Built in 1897, a modern wing was added in the mid-twentieth century. The hotel was well maintained and decorated in a traditional period style. It was seasonal, only operating for about six months of the year, which, of course, I was aware of, and I would be given other responsibilities during its closed period. The staff consisted largely of employees who had been there every season for many years, so they were very familiar with the property and those regular guest who came to Kenmare every year for their annual holiday. Many of these guests were from a generation that used to come by train before the diminution of the rail service. These were interspersed with some younger families and a smattering of American tourists.

Kenmare is a very pretty town nestled among the hills of Kerry, about thirty kilometres from Killarney and located on the Kenmare River which flowed gently through the edge of the village. Unlike in later years, when the town became much busier, in the seventies, it was very quiet, with three small hotels, a few guest houses, some tea rooms, and one particularly renowned restaurant, the Purple Heather, a place where Shelley and I would go for dinner when a break from the Great Southern Hotel was needed.

While we received a friendly welcome from the staff, it must be said that Shelley was somewhat of a novelty. This was Co. Kerry in the seventies, where Indians were a rarity. The warmth and friendliness of her personality soon overcame any strangeness, and she became well respected and liked.

On the five-acre grounds of the hotel were two small bungalows which were also used as guest accommodations. One of these was reassigned as the manager's bungalow, and we moved in after the introductions were completed. It consisted of two bedrooms, a kitchenette, a living room, and one bathroom. While small, it was adequately furnished and very comfortable.

I quickly settled into my responsibilities, much of which were in the tradition of 'mein host', a role that was very new to me, given my background in a major international chain of large hotels in major cities. My experience, however, stood me in good stead administratively, and the hotel completed my first season as its manager very successfully.

Erika started that September of 1976 in the local primary school, and we began to enjoy our new experience of country life and the village of Kenmare. A certain prestige accrued to being manager of the Great Southern Hotel, which had been an institution in Kenmare for about eighty years, and so I and my family were treated with a certain deference within the village. Shelley and Erika took up horse riding at a local stable, and on one such occasion, Erika became enthralled with a newly born puppy dog there. Much begging and pleading from her led to the acquisition of the puppy, and it soon became apparent that the appropriate name for him was 'Smarty'. He was a border collie and became a great source of both pleasure and, indeed, no small degree of wonder. He was unquestionably an incredibly smart animal, with behaviours that caused both amusement and, on occasions, concern or annoyance.

During that time, there was a TV commercial for a popular brand of sausages, and when it came on as we sat in the evenings watching TV, Smarty, upon hearing the musical jingle, would charge into the living room and sit in front of the TV, staring at it until the commercial ended, when he would retreat to whereever he was previously. When he wanted to have a bath, he would go to the bathroom, sit in the bathtub, and howl for attention. When he was naughty and being reproached for his behaviour, he would run and hide under a bed, or under the cupboard that was in the hallway.

On one occasion, there was an unhappy incident that was cause for concern. I was driving in the grounds of the hotel, and Smarty, while chasing the car, which he liked to do, was caught by the front wheels. He was badly bruised but otherwise unhurt. I felt that would teach him a lesson and, hopefully, end the bad habit of chasing cars. It didn't; it only stopped him chasing my car, as he continued to chase others.

The hotel's season ended in October, and as I prepared to see the last of the guests leave and begin the close-down procedures for the winter, I received instruction from head office to manage the Torc Great Southern Hotel in Killarney over the Christmas period as its manager was on leave.

However prior to that, in November, I was to reopen my hotel for three weeks for a film company who would shoot scenes for the movie *The Purple Taxi*. The hotel would remain closed to the public and the guest list would include the stars of the movie, Fred Astaire, Peter Ustinov, and Charlotte Rampling, along with the director and the rest of the crew. In due course, the film crew, stars, and support staff arrived at the hotel. Charlotte Rampling's young son and his nanny accompanied the actress, so they were given the second bungalow next to the manager's, and the rest of the cast and crew were accommodated in the hotel.

As shooting began for the movie, many of the hotel's staff were recruited as extras, and the hotel itself featured prominently. It was an exciting time for all, who had the opportunity to both meet and work with famous stars. The cast included Fred Astair who was famous for his dancing and singing partnership with Ginger Rogers in the forties and fifties. He was rather elderly at this stage and tended to spend time privately. Conversly, Peter Ustinov was great fun. He was extremely sociable and spent much of his time when 'off set' entertaining the staff with his endless amusing tales and jokes. He was in real life just as he appeared in his movies, big, funny, and enormously good humoured. When Shelley decided to ask him for his autograph he enquired as to whom he should address it.

"To Shelley" she replied. Looking at her he said,

" It must be something more exotic than that"

" My Indian name is RajLaxmi"

" Oh! Too complicated it'll have to be Shelley then". He responded with a hugh belly laugh.

The 'shooting' lasted about a month, my family and I along with the staff enjoyed a memoriable experience and all where sorry to see our trip into fantasy land end. The stars and crew departed, and the hotel closed down for the season.

The staff left until the following spring, and we moved to the Torc Great Southern in Killarney to prepare for the Christmas season. That Christmas, the Torc Hotel hosted a successful Christmas package, with a full house for the period. The festivities continued through New Year, culminating in a lavish New Year's Eve dinner and dance and, finally, New Year's Day buffet.

The manager of the Torc returned in early January, and we went back to Kenmare. It was time to start planning for the upcoming season of 1977 that would begin around April. Budgets had to be made, staffing guides developed, and staff interviews planned, along with activities and entertainment organised.

In early February, I received a phone call to come to Dublin for a meeting. As it was outside the regular meeting routine, which consisted of a monthly trip for all the company's hotel managers to Dublin, I was curious.

"Ok, what's it about"? I asked the hotel operations director who was on the other end of the line

"I can't say right now. It'll have to wait 'til you get here," was the rather curt response. He apparently did not want to be drawn into any discussion about the subject matter, so the conversation ended abruptly.

On the appointed date, I drove to Killarney and boarded the early train to Dublin. As on other occasions when I would go for the monthly managers meeting with the four other Kerry hotel managers, I went to the first-class carriage and settled in, and as the journey began, ordered a full breakfast to sustain me. The only difference on this occasion was that I was alone, so whatever this mysterious meeting was about, it obviously did not concern any of my other Kerry colleagues.

On arriving in Dublin, I headed for Restaurant Na Mara in Dun Laoire, which was owned by Great Southern Hotels and where the company's head office was located. I was not the only one summoned, as the managers from the Mulranny, Sligo, and Bundoran hotels were also in attendance. Pre-meeting conversations speculated on why the four of us had been summoned. What was to come was an unexpected and unwelcome bombshell.

The meeting commenced, with the operations director, reading from a prepared script:

"As a result of the oil crises of the seventies and the downturn in tourism due to the Northern Ireland Troubles, the Great Southern Group finds itself in financial difficulty. In 1977, the company will sell the Kenmare, Mulranny, Sligo, and Bundoran hotels to the private sector to raise capital for essential refurbishment of the remaining hotels. As of now, there are no plans to open for the season, and as there are no positions for senior managers available within the company, you will be made redundant. You will be paid redundancy in accordance with your length of service. Details will be sent to you in writing"

With that, the meeting ended with no questions entertained and details of the severance to follow. And I, along with three of my collegues was out of a job, an ignominious end to what I thought would be a long career with a relatively small but sound national hotel company. I had sacrificed my career with InterContinental Hotels, one of the world largest and most prestigious hotel companies, on the altar of impatience and the need for instant gratification. My demons surfacing!

The return journey to Kenmare that day was an unhappy one. I faced the undesirable prospect of informing Shelley that we would again be on the move, and this time without knowing to where or what the future might hold. I also did not relish the thought of telling Erika that she would be parted from newly made friends, this for the fourth time in her very young life. Even at her young age, I sensed she resented being brought from place to place and school to school. But pragmatic, not emotional thinking was now required, and the anguish and disappointment at the current state of affairs must be replaced with a plan to move forward and seek employment wherever it may be.

I was a positive thinker, and soon, the negativity was dispelled with the belief that a better role would be forthcoming. We were permitted to stay in the manager's bungalow for the foreseeable future, or until the hotel sale was completed. Although relatively small because of my short service with the company, the redundancy payment would keep us 'whole' for some time while I sought new opportunities.

Back in Kenmare, Shelley, although greatly disappointed, handled the bad news with the inherent belief that she always exhibited: " If it was meant to be, something better will come along." Erika's disappointment was, unfortunately, a double dose. She also had to part with Smarty, her dog. She had wanted him as a puppy earlier, but he had grown quickly, and as a dog bred for sheep herding and open farmland, it would be unfair to confine him to lesser spaces. We were forced to give him away, and that, for Erika, was heart breaking, as she was not only attached to Smarty, but showed great concern for animals in general, always wanting to bring home any cats or dogs she thought might need tender loving care. We identified a local farmer who was very happy to give Smarty a home, and when Erika understood that he would be more content in that environment, she accepted the decision with good grace.

My extensive history with InterContinental Hotels in Africa, Asia, and Europe, my education in Cornell, my management training in Germany, and opening experiences at the Dacca, Nairobi, and at the London InterContinental, along with my role in London as cost controller, was very likely unique in the Irish hotel scene at the time. With patience, time, and a measured and careful management of the job search, it was possible that a 'plum' position would become available in due course. But true to character, the burden of my impatient nature, coupled with the concern that there were now also three other Great Southern Hotel managers in the job market, drove my decision to accept the first hotel manager's position that was offered, and so I did exactly that. While time and the insignificance of the position in the overall history of the our family has dimmed the memory of all of the details of my next job, it would not be inaccurate to describe it as a horrendous error.

Early in April that year, 1977, I answered an ad in a national newspaper for the position of manager of the Montague Hotel, Portlaoise. It was located just outside the town on the main Dublin Road leading to the southern part of Ireland. It was described as a freestanding, sixty-bedroom, three-star property on its own grounds, with dining and banqueting facilities, catering mainly to business travellers and tourists for room business as well as locals for functions and weddings. I applied and was invited for an interview. On the appointed date, I drove from Kenmare to Portlaoise. My initial impression of the hotel was not entirely unfavourable. It was a modern building, rather functional, with little architectural merit, yet not exactly unattractive, and it seemed clean and well maintained. I advised the front desk staff that I was here for an interview and was shown to an office, where I met the hotel's owner. There was a second gentleman present, who was introduced as the owner's accountant. He questioned me extensively on my accounting knowledge and while I explained that I was quite familiar with hotel accounting, I was not a chartered accountant. The accounting questions continued and the less knowledgable I was about more complex accounting procedures, the more pleased he seemed to be. Rather strange! Following the interview, we had lunch, toured the hotel and the manager's house that was on the grounds, and bid our farewells. I returned to Kenmare to await their decision. On my drive home that day, I pondered the questions asked in the interview, particularly the financial ones, and the strange reaction to my inability to answer some.

Shortly after the interview, I received a phone call from the owner offering me the position of hotel manager, which I was happy to accept, although still puzzled by some of the interview questions. We packed up the car, the new Ford Cortina, which I had purchased before the 'hammer was lowered' on my job with Great Southern Hotels, and departed Kenmare.

Upon arrival at the hotel, we were met by the owner's accountant and brought to the manager's house, where we could unload the car and settle in. I left Shelley to organise the house while I went to meet the staff. Though the hotel itself, located outside a relatively small town in rural Ireland, was not my idea of the perfect property to be managing, it was a job, and I needed to work on improving both its reputation and profitability, so I set about the task of analysing its current and past business practices.

On the domestic front, an early task was to enrol Erika in school, this for the fifth time, and there is little that can be said about that as we recognized that five separate and distant schools in three different countries for a nine-year-old was already way too much. Many years later, as an adult, Erika would remind us of that fact. The school was in Portlaoise, and I would drive her there in the morning and collect her in the afternoon.

Based on what eventually transpired, it is probably prudent to minimise discourse on the details of subsequent events, but suffice to say that my tenure with this hotel was much shorter than ever anticipated. My eventual departure was precipitated by my commitment to my own honesty and integrity, along with the desire by the property's owner and his accountant to use the hotel for nefarious purposes, something they seemed to regard rather lightly.

As general manager, I was a signatory for the business, and as my first month on the job progressed, I became aware of the strangeness of financial recordings. The owner's accountant managed the finances of the hotel and I began to notice the daily sales reports did not reflect what was happening 'on the ground'. This caused me considerable concern and at the end of the month when asked to sign off on the financial statement I questioned the inflated sales and expense figures.

"Don't worry about it, that's my job, just sign off on it"; was the response. I now understood the financial questioning during the interview. It was designed to determine if I would understand what was going on or not.

While done very expertly, and I couldn't entirely be sure, but it appeared that funds may have been moved through the property's accounts that were not actual sales. I refused to participate in things I thought that the appropriate authorities might be particularly interested in. The end result of this situation was a request for my resignation, and this, I readily provided, one month after I started as the hotel's manager.

While I was again unemployed, I valued My integrity more than any singular position, and it was and would become a characteristic of mine, admired and respected by many others I was to know and work with throughout my life. So, it was 'back on the street', with no job and no home. There was no option but to impose ourselves on the generosity of my parent, so we called them to request an open-ended visit. Our request was readily granted, but whether they actually felt happy about this imposition, we would never know.

Again, we were forced to move and take Erika out of a school where she had just started; this whole exercise was becoming very troubling. I was determined that I would not move my family again until I was absolutely certain there was stability—well, as certain as certain can be.

Immediately upon returning to Stillorgan, I once more began the search for a position. As my concern now further heightened, I became even less cautious and ended up again taking the first position I was offered: general manager of the Hotel Royale in Monaghan, close to the border with Northern Ireland. The name of the hotel was not really Royale, but given where it was located and the nature of its clientele and other circumstance, which will become apparent, its real name is better left unacknowledged. The position was obtained in response to a newspaper advertisement, and sight unseen after an interview in Dublin, I accepted the job. On this occasion, I would go to Monaghan alone until it was decided that moving Shelley and Erika again, was appropriate.

So on the appointed day of joining the hotel, I drove to Monaghan, a couple of hours on the road. Leaving Dublin early that first Monday morning in June, I arrived in time to meet the owner and begin my first day on the job. I had not previously seen the hotel, but it was much the same in appearance, size, and style as the Hotel Montague I had left just a few short weeks earlier: sixty rooms, a bar, a restaurant, a ballroom, and a Saturday night dance, as was also held in the Hotel Montague. Maybe an ominous similarity?

Monaghan had a population of about seven thousand souls, and as there was no manager's accommodation at the hotel, we would eventually need to find a home in the town. *Is this what I'm reduced to, running nondescript cheap hotels in rural Ireland along the country roads of small towns?* The events of this year and the current prospect of managing this hotel were starting to take its toll on my sense of well-being, and my spirit began to wilt. *This whole situation is depressing.* Given the calibre of the hotel and it's clientele, it was very difficult to stay positive. By this time in my career, I had been involved for over a decade on the management teams of major international hotels on three continents and in large and renowned cities. This place I was now in, both physically and mentally, was a new low for me, and I felt it deeply, but I had a family to support and needed to remain positive no matter how difficult that was. So, I set about the task of reviewing the hotel and its business practices.

My first week I would devoted to familiarization. This being the mid-seventies, when peace, intercommunity understanding, and the so-called 'Good Friday Agreement' were in the distant future, and three years earlier, Monaghan had suffered through a horrific terrorist bomb that killed seven people. A certain general suspicion, warranted or not, seemed pervasive wherever people gathered. With Monaghan's geographic location jutting into Northern Ireland, some of the clients that frequented the hotel's rather dated bar, who drank either alone or in small male groups engaged in deep conversation, elicited thoughts of who they might be, or what they were about. Muddy boots, peaked caps, and turned-up coat collars epitomised the dress of much of the clientele. As time passed, my belief in both my willingness and, indeed, my ability to run this business began to diminish.

The big event for the hotel each week was the Saturday night dinner dance, and by all accounts from staff I spoke with, it was very popular, always attracting a packed ballroom accommodating about two hundred people. I felt that with those numbers, it would be a perfect occasion to re-energise the hotel's sagging restaurant and banquet business. In discussions with the 'chef' and service personnel, I set about upgrading the food, service, and overall quality of the experience, which would hopefully result in positive word of-mouth-marketing. As it transpired, I failed in my market research. While referred to by staff and locals as 'the dinner dance', it was less so in the usually recognized sense, but more a 'supper dance', where the one and only fare served during a halftime interval from the music was a chicken and chip plate on paper plates with plastic cutlery, followed by a desert of a small ice cream tub.

On the night of the new 'dinner dance', there were clothed tables, real crockery, and regular cutlery. The menu consisted of a choice of two dishes, one of chicken nicely sauced and the other of fish, both accompanied by a sauté or au gratin potato and a fresh vegetable, and for all this, the entry price remained the same. And no chips!

The crowds arrived, the men still peak-capped and booted, although the mud was removed, and the boots were polished. The girls' dress sense was 'rural' in style, and the dancing, when it started, was indescribable. There was just one more action that night that would confirm my ever-growing conviction that this was indeed 'wild frontier country', and it was about to descend upon me with the full force of unfettered anger. The music stopped, and dinner was served, and that was when the trouble started. There were no chips! The menu that had been prepared was not appreciated, and the shouting and counter-arguments began. I was accosted.

"No fucking chips? What's this shit?" This was started by one or two more vocal souls, but soon, the mantra was taken up by many. "No chips!" "No fucking chips!" "What's this shit!" "What a fucking dump!" and a lot more commentary was hurled at me, much at very close quarter, by large and angry peaked caps. Frozen chips were rescued from the fridge and quickly presented to the deep fat fryer, and some degree of order was restored. This was the proverbial 'straw that broke the camel's back', and it confirmed my earlier feeling that this was not the place for me.

The dance ended at two am Sunday morning, and after I had supervised the clean-up and seen the last of the staff of the premises, I set about finalising my departure. I completed the documentation on the night's business, wrote a resignation letter, placed that along with the hotel keys in an envelope addressed to the owner, left it on top of the desk, and locked the office. I went to my room, packed my bags, and drove off the hotel parking lot for the last time. It was four a.m. Sunday morning, June 12, 1977, seven days after I'd started, and I was exhausted, physically, mentally, and even spiritually, and very likely, if there was any other possible way to be exhausted, I was. I fell asleep at the wheel. Minutes later, I instinctively awoke with a start just as the car was moving quickly on the wrong side of the road and heading for a ditch. As it was very early on a Sunday morning, I was fortunate there was no other traffic on the road. I drove into a lay-by and napped for about an hour before resuming the drive to Dublin.

No one at my parent's house knew I was on the way there, as my decision to walk away from the hotel was taken at the conclusion of the Saturday dance the previous night, or rather, early that morning. My discontent during the seven days was, of course, building to that decision, but I never let it be known to Shelley that I was unhappy. My arrival would be unexpected and the circumstances unwelcome, as I was again jobless.

As was expected, I was in time for breakfast. Surprise and

disappointment bordering on mild shock greeted me as I arrived at the front door of the house in Stillorgan. This disappointment, the third of the year, accompanied by the need to once more impose ourselves on the generosity of my parents for accommodation, was beginning too seriously depress me, and I feared for my mental stability.

Johnny Browne, a former colleague of mine when we worked at the InterContinental Hotel in Dublin some years earlier, was now employed by Bord Failte, the Irish Tourism Board. At that time, the Northern Ireland Tourist Authority and Bord Failte worked closely together in order to promote tourism to the Island of Ireland as a whole, intended as a positive countermeasure to the negative publicity caused by political instability in the North. Johnny and I still maintained some contact, albeit infrequently. Very shortly after my departure from Monaghan, I received a phone call from him.

"Hi Colm, listen, I know about the Hotel in Kenmare being up for sale. What's happening with you?"

" I'm out of a job, I'm afraid", was my simple response.

My brief time at the hotels in Port Laoise and Monaghan, while certainly an experience from which some valuable lessons were learned, contributed nothing to my resume. Thus they were confined to oblivion, never to surface in conversation.

"Colm, I'm working on some stuff with the Tourism Board of Northern Ireland, and I wanted to give you a heads up. Dunadry Inn, one of the top hotels up there, recently lost their general manager. If you'r interested I'll give you the contact details, and then it's up to you." Said Johnny.

Before the advent of 'the information super highway', as the internet was first appropriately named, research was considerably more difficult, so I needed to physically go through the process of meeting the 'players', seeing the property, and reviewing its background before I would make any decision. I finally, realized I needed to be much more careful than in the recent past. So, time to make contact. I phoned Mr. Paddy Faloon, the owner of the hotel, expressed my interest, and asked if I could submit my resume for consideration. Following a cordial and encouraging phone conversation with Mr. Faloon, I was invited to come to his country house in Co Kildare to meet him.

Finding the house was not difficult, as inquiries from locals in the vicinity led me to its exact location. It was obvious that the house was well known. And that was unsurprising, for as I came upon it, I was astounded. I drove through large, wrought-iron gates and along a long gravel drive flanked by grassland and trees, ending in front of what could only be described as a 'stately home'. It was impressive, a three-storey Georgian-style house facing south, with two single-storied curved wings reaching out from each side like wecoming arms. One east wing and one west wing. My first thought was, *This is the home of a wealthy person. His hotel must be very profitable.* Actually, it wasn't, but Paddy Faloon was wealthy.

The massive front door was opened to my knock by what appeared to be an employee, a young woman dressed in business style.

"Hello, I'm Colm Madden. I have an appoint with Mr. Faloon."

"Yes, we're expecting you. Please, come in. I'll show you to the library, and Mr. Faloon will be with you shortly."

She did not provide her name.

Paddy Faloon was probably at that time in his sixties. He was very elegant and very much an 'Irish country gentleman'. He was a protestant from Northern Ireland, but was 'completely Irish', as distinct from 'Northern Irish'. He lived in his magnificent house in Kildare, but also maintained a large house on the grounds of Dunadry Inn, his hotel in Co Antrim in Northern Ireland, which he used on his frequent visits to the inn. Mr. Faloon provided me with all the information I needed to feel positive about the company and the hotel. I learned that the hotel had made no profit for many years and that a return to profitability would be generously rewarded. I learned that the Faloon family were not dependent on Dunadry Inn for their wealth, as they also owned the Northern Brick Company, a very successful, large brick manufacturing company, as well as considerable farming interests in Northern Ireland. Faloon was impressed with my background. Subject to a visit to the hotel, the agreement of his managing director, Colin Noble, and his son Neil, who was a director of the company, the position of general manager of the Dunadry Inn was mine.

Arrangements were made for the visit, so approximately a week later, Shelley and I set out on the three-hour drive to Templepatrick, Co Antrim, the village in which Dunadry Inn was located. We crossed the border at Newry, Co Down, and entered Northern Ireland, both of us for the first time ever. We felt an immediate change in the air, a sense of tension. The presence of British military was evident everywhere. Armoured vehicles patrolled the streets and the highways as we drove toward our destination. We were stopped on several occasions at either police or army checkpoints. It was just a little uncomfortable, but since we had been through serious security situations on a number of previous occasions, we would not be deterred from our quest by 'the troubles' here in Northern Ireland.

At the entrance to the hotel, the gate was closed and manned by security guards, who checked our identities and searched the car. Satisfied we were legitimate and not possible members of one of the Catholic or Protestant paramilitary groups prevalent in Northern Ireland at that time, we were granted entry to the parking lot.

First impressions were very positive. The hotel was a four-star property converted from an old mill, had mountains of character and could appropriately be describe as up-market boutique style.

The main entrance was through a rotunda tower, opening onto a large lounge area with a great stone fireplace as its focal point at one end, a small bar at the opposite end, and a reception desk to the side. The place exuded a warm, welcoming feel with its live peat-burning fire, its polished wooden floor covered in antique Persian carpets, and its perimeter furnished with antique church pews, upholstered for comfort. It was evident the hotel was a labour of love for Mr. Faloon, and this opinion would continue to be reinforced later when we toured the property. It was an enormously improved change from the previous two properties I had become involved with.

We checked into the room where we would stay for a couple of nights while I was in discussion with Colin Noble and Neal Faloon. The staff was well trained, efficient, and courteous, and I was feeling very positive for the first time since my departure from Kenmare. I hoped that the discussions to take place would confirm me as the general manager of this fine property. We had dinner that evening in the hotel restaurant, an excellent meal chosen from a well-balanced and interesting menu, best described as classical continental, and the quality of the food suggested a knowledgeable chef.

Next morning after breakfast, I went with one of the reception staff to meet with Colin Noble and Neal Faloon. Their offices were located in a separate building on the extensive grounds of the hotel, close to Paddy Faloon's second home. Both the farming interests and the Northern Brick Company businesses were conducted out of this office, and Colin Noble was managing director of the group. Introductions were made, and the interview began. Right from the start, it didn't seem to go so well, with Noble expressing doubts about my general management experience. He referred to my position as cost controller in the London InterContinental as a "limited-administration-type role". He also felt that less than a year as manger in the Great Southern Hotel was insufficient, and he seemed to minimise the extensive people management skills I had developed over my years in Europe, Africa, and Asia with InterContinental Hotels Corp. I responded knowledgeably to their questions, but the coolness and lack of enthusiasm in the room was keenly felt by me. The meeting ended without the confirmation I was hoping for, but a promise that I would hear from them in a few days with their decision.

We returned to Dublin immediately after the meeting, decidedly less cheerful than on the drive up to Dunadry the day before, when I felt that Paddy Faloon's approval of me was a nod to the affirmative. Now I thought that might have been a misread!

Two days later, the doubt turned to reality when Colin Noble phoned me to thank me for my interest, but they had appointed someone else to the position. To be a fly on the wall wherever the conversation about this situation had taken place between Paddy Faloon, owner and chairman, and Colin Noble, his managing director, would have been an interesting experience. That was an afterthought, though, and certainly, at the time, it was not on my mind. I was once again disappointed. The tunnel of my despair darkened, with no light at its end.

What to do, where to go, how to find my way back? Pray a little, so I did! While I believe that one's religion or lack thereof is their own business, without meaning to sound glib, but to briefly rationalise why prayer; I might loosly describe myself as a liberal conservative Catholic, maybe a paradox. I believed divorce should be allowed, married priests were acceptable, and gay people were born that way. My conservatism guided my belief that abortion was wrong, evil was real, a spirit world existed, honouring the Sabath was the right thing to do, and prayer worked. So against this backdrop of ingrained belief, prayer was now the one thing left to me.

"Colm, phone call for you" my father called out to me about a month later. It was early August as we sat at the dining table over dinner.

" It's Mr. Paddy Faloon."

"Colm, I hope you're still available,".

"Yes I am".

"Excellent, I want to offer you the position. In spite of my decision to choose you, my two directors thought they knew best and hired a drunk. They've now had to physically put him on a plane and send him back to England. We'll make sure the compensation package is generous. I hope you'll accept."

"Absolutely, very happy to, Mr Faloon, I loved the hotel and thank you.".

I felt a wave of relief, and excitement roll over me. It was the beginning of what might poetically be described as my 'Midas Touch' period. For the next four years, nothing would go wrong, and everything I touched would turn to 'metaphorical gold', as it were. By the end of my first year as general manager of Dunadry Inn, I was appointed to the board of directors. By the end of my second year, business was so good the company decided to construct an additional forty guest rooms.

While I was very grateful to my parents for having allowed us to stay with them during this troubled year, I hoped that as we set off for Antrim and my new position, we would never have to ask for such assistance again. And we never did!

Several old cottages which had been carefully and tastefully renovated along with two larger modern bungalows were provided for the accommodation of several senior staff, and upon our arrival at Dunadry Inn, we were allocated one of those cottages.

Over the coming days and after, all introductions were completed and we began to settle in to our new life. I set about the task of reviewing the business of the hotel and its profit potential. With active, intelligent marketing strategies geared to several operational changes, business began to quickly improve. By the completion of the first financial year under my management,

Dunadry Inn made a profit for the first time in many years. This was reported in January 1979 for the year 1978. Rather than take my generous bonus all in cash, which would increase my tax burden, I accepted Mr. Faloon's two-year-old BMW 3.0 in part payment. Mr. Faloon changed his vehicles frequently. I sold my one-year-old Ford Cortina for cash, thus acquiring an upgraded luxury vehicle and non-taxable cash, a good financial end to year one at 'The Inn'.

The accolades poured in, and just two months after I started the company confirmed my appointment and moved us from the cottage into the larger of the two bungalows, designated as the general manager's official residence. My reputation quickly grew, and in October of 1977, the British Institute of Management, who had selected Dunadry Inn for their annual conference, were profuse in their praise. Following the BIM conference, in November, the Northern Ireland Tourist Board selected Dunadry Inn to host a dinner for senior American-based executives of Aer Lingus touring the island of Ireland. We served 1945 vintage Taylor port and 1961 Chateau Latour, which I had discovered in the hotel's wine cellar, complemented by food equally as impressive.

In January 1978, I was invited to give two presentations to the student body at Ulster College, the Northern Ireland polytechnic. In the Mouton Cadet menu competition of 1978, which compares the menus of hotel restaurants and free-standing restaurants throughout Europe, Dunadry Inn won second prize for the Northern Ireland region, beaten only by what was generally recognized as the best free-standing restaurant in the province. In 1978, Dunadry Inn also had the highest sales of one of its beer suppliers, and in recognition, I was awarded a weeklong, all-expenses paid golf trip to Majorca. While I didn't play golf, I went minus clubs to enjoy sun, sea, sand and sangria.

By this time we were well settled in Dunadry, and Erika was

happy at the tiny Lawther primary school, where Mr. Bunting was principal, assisted by Ms. Goode. Erika would move from the primary school to Antrim Grammar School at the start of the school year in September 1979.

The second full year, 1979, of our time in Dunadry evolved into a particularly busy one, both personally and professionally. The social highlight for Dunadry Inn, and indeed much of the area, was the annual May Ball. It was a lavish affair hosted by the hotel in support of the local Lions Club. Champagne flowed, and extensive buffet tables creaked under a virtual cornucopia of gourmet food. The hotel entrance was decorated with a lavish arch of flowers, and the tables were dressed with linens in the Lions Club colours of blue and gold. The resident band played music to dance to, and a variety of acts entertained the guests. As general manager, I hosted a private room for pre-dinner drinks, and a few of our close friends, along with my two sisters and their husbands, traveled from Dublin to Dunadry for the weekend of the ball.

At the end of that year, when my bonus was calculated, the income tax burden was unhappily unwelcome, so I requested the company to sell me the manager's bungalow, reducing the price by the amount of my bonus. This, they agreed to do.

In 1979, the England football team, for their game against Northern Ireland, stayed at Dunadry Inn, and *The Sunday Times* based their reporters at the hotel. Business continued to increase, guests were happy, and we began building the additional forty guest bedrooms. In October of 1978, construction began on the DeLorean car manufacturing plant in Dunmurray, and in early 1979, the company executives began to arrive in the province. Many of them initially stayed in Dunadry Inn, including Brian Beharrell, his wife, Bette, and their two daughters, Susan and Lynette, both girls about Erika's age. Brian was the CIO, chief information officer for DeLorean and had recently joined the company from South Africa.

While I recognized Brian and his family as guests of the hotel, our friendship was born after a Sunday lunch over bottles of good wine from Dunadry's cellar and new South African wines that Brian had brought with him, as yet relatively unknown in Northern Ireland. The conviviality cemented our friendship, and even at that early stage, we agreed to combine efforts and fulfil the lifelong sailing dreams we both shared. We decided that Sunday afternoon, undoubtedly fuelled by the copious amounts of wine consumed, to jointly purchase a sailing yacht, and subsequently, over the next few weeks, we set about the search.

Eventually, after a month, the Beharrell family moved out of the hotel into their own home, and shortly thereafter, I received a phone call from Brian.

"Hi Colm, how about a brand new Westerly 33 Twin-Keeled Ketch,".

"Sounds great, where is it"?

"It's a demonstration boat in Westerly's yard in Southampton, for sale at twenty five thousand pounds, I think, we should go for it", responded Brian. After receiving pictures, brochures, and spec. sheets, we decided to buy the Westerly, which we eventually named *Shebe*.

Our friends Maggie and Cyril from Syria, were now retired back in England and were in occasional contact with us. Cyril had taken up sailing, was a keen dingy sailor, and was interested in joining Brian and I on the voyage from Southampton back to Strangford Lough in Northern Ireland, where we would lay down a permanent mooring for *Shebe*. Early summer that year, Cyril and Maggie came to Dunadry, and while Maggie stayed with Shelley and Erika, Brian, Cyril and I travelled to Southampton to take possession of the Westerly 33. While all three of us had sailed small boats, none had been offshore. In the days before GPS existed or was available to the general public, navigation was a more complex exercise, so we hired a two-man delivery crew to sail with us back to Northern

Ireland.

With the ship's papers in our possession and bank accounts emptied, we set sail from Southampton early on a Monday in June. Sailing out of the Solent, we planned to continue non-stop to Northern Ireland, a distance of about 580 nautical miles. If we could average five knots, the journey should take about five days. The sea was mirror like as we left, you could see your reflection in the still waters. As the morning wore on and the wind increased in tandem with the growing seas, I quickly recognised that Cyril was extremely prone to seasickness. By mid-afternoon, he became very ill, and some hours later, he was so debilitated that he was unable to remain upright and could only lie in his bunk. We became concerned over his condition, and although still some considerable distance away, we elected to break the journey and sail into Falmouth Harbour to rest and consider seeking medical assistance. It has been known that in extreme cases, severe seasickness can even lead to death.

We were into the second day of our voyage by the time we reached Falmouth, and Cyril's condition had improved slightly, enough for us to pick up a mooring and go ashore for a meal. Cyril had not eaten since we'd started out the previous morning and needed to regain his strength. We spent the night on the mooring to help his recovery and made several attempts at encouraging him to discontinue the journey, take a train to London, and fly back to Belfast, where we would meet him upon our arrival, but to no avail: he insisted on continuing and would not be talked out of that decision. Because of Cyril's condition and his unwillingness to leave the voyage, we decided to do the remainder of the journey in stages, and the following morning, set sail across the Irish Sea to Wexford, then to Dublin, where we rested, and then on Strangford Lough, arriving after six days. We felt jelly-legged stepping onto dry land after the journey, but were pleased to arrive safely with Cyril, although quite ill, quickly recovering. Following a few days' rest and recovery, Cyril and Maggie returned home in England.

Next on our agenda was a summer holiday we'd arranged during the month of August when Padma, Shelley's younger sister, came to visit us in Northern Ireland, and a trip around Europe was planned. So, I traded in the BMW 3.0 for a new BMW 520, rented a trailer tent, hooked it up to the car, and set off on the car ferry from Larne to Stranraer. We were away for three weeks, driving through England, France, Spain, Switzerland, and Germany, camping in the trailer tent, eating in cafes or in campsites, and enjoying the experience of the simple pleasures of a nomadic lifestyle. Eventually, the holiday ended, we returned to Northern Ireland, and Padma left for her home.

Lest we forget we lived in Northern Ireland in the time of a troubled society, in early February 1980, an incident shook our complacency to remind us that danger could rear its ugly head at any time. One evening, a heavily pregnant women checked into the hotel alone. She checked out the following morning considerably less pregnant, but at the busy reception desk, nobody noticed. Around eleven a.m. that morning, I received a phone call from the executive housekeeper.

"Mr. Madden, can you please come to Room 114? We have a problem."

Upon arriving at the room, I was overcome by a powerful odour of petrol, and looking for the source, I noticed a package under the bed. I immediately had the room locked down and phoned the police. They determined the package looked extremely suspicious, but it was outside their sphere of knowledge or responsibility, so they called the army, who sent a bomb disposal squad.

"We need to immediately evacuate everyone from the hotel, staff and guests", the officer in charge instructed me and of course, I willingly complied.

Having the staff round up the guests to leave the hotel and

gather in the parking lot outside in the cold of an Irish winter's morning while keeping the information about what was happening as discrete as possible proved a challenge. It was no secret that dangerous incidents were always a possibility in Northern Ireland in those days. Dunadry Inn, although having a high profile, was rarely impacted due to its rural location. However, the possibility of snowballing news around the community that there might be a bomb in the inn would still be very unwelcome.

Offloaded from the rear of the truck in which the military arrived was a small vehicle that could not have been more than about one foot wide, and two in length, possibly nine or ten inches in height that resembled a small army tank. One of the soldiers donned a heavily padded suit and large helmet with facemask, while a rope was attached to his waist. With a handheld control unit, he set the 'mini-tank' in motion, following it toward room 114. Tense staff and guests gathered in the parking lot during the thirty minutes or so the officer was out of sight. It was now obvious to all what the request for evacuation was about.

A muted conversation on the radio took place between the soldier inside and officer in charge. Subsequently, guests and staff were moved to the far end of the parking lot as the soldier emerged through the hotel front entrance carrying the package, which he then placed inside a large box-like container on the truck. They dismantled their equipment and advised me that everything was now okay and that they would dispose of the item and all could re-enter the hotel. They later confirmed it was an explosive device wrapped in a hot water bottle filled with petrol. The consequence of this item being detonated would have unquestionably led to one of the worst disasters during those times in Northern Ireland. This information was not shared with either guests or staff, who were advised that it was a suspicious package and everything was quite safe. The staff was instructed not to further discuss this incident. They diligently complied, and it was never mentioned again.

When I first accepted the position with Dunadry Inn in 1977, my parents had been concerned that we were placing ourselves in danger, but the incident almost three years later with the bomb was the only lapse in safety during our entire time in Dunadry. Secure in the knowledge that they would be safe, they decided to visit for a week in the spring of 1980. After their short holiday was concluded, they returned to Dublin, happily impressed by the warmth and friendliness of the people they had met during their stay.

During the sailing season from May to October, *Shebe*, our sailing yacht, was shared between ourselves and the Beharrell family, each of whom would have use of it every alternate weekend, along with whatever other time we wished that was agreed upon by both families. In August that year, Shelley and I invited Erika's friend Louise Cowman to join us for our first long family trip onboard *Shebe*. We sailed out of Strangford Lough on a blustery morning with the sea just slightly less than angry and a sky suggesting the onslaught of heavy showers at best, or a continuously miserable day at worst. We had provisioned the boat the previous night and slept aboard. Louise and Erika were fast asleep in the aft cabin as I weighed anchor and *Shebe* charged through the ever-building seas. The two girls were soon on deck, both with a greenish pallor, which quickly led to relieving the contents of their stomachs over the side. Shortly thereafter, however, as breakfast settled queasy tummies, the early morning sun broke through the clouds, and the seas settled down, the thrill of the sail soon lifted everyone's spirit.

We headed south to Dun Laoire, our first port of call, arriving by evening. Unlike the present day, when there is a sizeable marina in Dun Laoire, in those days, there was just a handful of sailboats on moorings in the inner harbour, so I tied up *Shebe* alongside the harbour wall, close to a ladder that would allow easy access on and off the boat, as the tidal range is around two and a half metres. We planned to spend one or two nights there before continuing the voyage, and we invited any of the family to a meal onboard. Dymphna and Ronnie, my sister and brother-in-law accepted and came aboard at high tide.

Following a couple of days in Dun Laoire, we sailed out of the harbour and headed for Wicklow. It was a gorgeous morning, with a steady breeze and a clear sky. It was a short journey of only a few hours, and the expectation was we would arrive in time for lunch. With little warning, the weather soon changed, the sails where shortened, and very quickly, as gusts rose above twenty-five knots, I took the sails down completely except for a tiny triangle of mainsail, and *Shebe* flew along towards Wicklow at speeds touching seven knots. The remainder of the trip was uneventful as the sailing conditions continued to be perfect. From Wicklow to Wexford harbour, we went, and then back to Howth, where we picked up a mooring, prepared dinner, and had an early night. We planned to sail the following morning directly to Strangford Lough.

While it was still dark, Shelley and I arose from our bunk as dawn was breaking. Shelley prepared breakfast, I slipped the mooring. and we quietly left Howth Harbour under power on a flat, calm sea. We expected to be on the mooring in Strangford Lough before dark that evening. The tide runs through the narrows in and out of the Lough extremely fast, up to four knots, so we timed it to arrive on a rising tide; otherwise, we would not get in. A stiff, constant breeze allowed us to carry full sail all day as *Shebe* scooted happily along, and as planned, we caught the strong incoming tide and charged through the narrows into the expanse of Strangford Lough, picked up the mooring, offloaded everything onto the dingy, rowed ashore, loaded up the car, and headed home to Dunadry. We were both feeling happy, we had successfully accomplished our first sailing holiday aboard our Westerly 33 ketch.

Both we and the Beharrell family continued to sail *Shebe* well into the autumn, sometimes alternating weekend and sometimes all sailing together. Our family's final sail of 1980 was a weekend in late September to the Isle of Man, and little did we realise at that time that it would be our last trip aboard our beloved *Shebe*. In mid-October, as the winter approached, the boat was hauled ashore at a boatyard in the Lough, covered with its tarpaulin, and left to rest until the following spring.

Shortly afterwards, while at work one day, I had a visit from the Northern Ireland representative for the Moet et Chandon vineyard. "Colm in recognition of the incredible sales of Moet et Chandon and Dom Perignon Champagnes at Dunadry Inn over the past two years, the company would like to invite you for a weekend to their chateau in France. They'll send their company jet to Belfast airport and fly you and five others to Reims on a weekend of your choice." Because Dunadry Inn had done so well in the sale of wines and Champagnes during my years there, I had received several gifts from suppliers, but this was exceptional. I suggested a weekend in October, hoping the weather would still be considerate before winter arrived.

On the appointed Friday morning of our departure, a Mercedes limousine arrived at the hotel to take me to the Airport, a mere fifteen-minute drive. It was permitted directly onto a portion of the tarmac allocated for private planes, where it pulled up in front of a luxurious private jet. I was escorted aboard by the plane's attractive hostess, who was elegantly attired in a uniform with a crest indicating she was an employee of Moet et Chandon. Five more limousines arrived in a similar fashion, with two members of the Irish agents of Moet et Chandon, another hotelier, and two restaurateurs, all whom I knew. We boarded, the plane, it took off, soon reaching a cruising altitude over forty-thousand feet, well above commercial traffic. The time to Reims was about two hours, and hors d'oeuvres and Champagne were served in abundance throughout the flight. The sensation was thrilling, and comparing the experience to flying in a commercial airliner, would be like comparing a sports car to a bus.

Landing in Reims, we alighted from the plane and were met by the major domo of the Chateau Moet et Chandon and escorted to limousines that were directly on the tarmac. We were then driven approximately thirty kilometres through beautiful vineyard-covered rolling landscapes to Epernay, the home of Moet et Chandon.

Moet et Chandon is by far the biggest of the Champagne houses, and until 1962, when it became a *"société anonyme"*, it was one of the largest business in France owned by a single family. Producer of the famed luxury champagne Dom Perignon, it is the world's largest producer of Champagne, having more than two thousand acres under 'the vine'. The company also owns many French luxury brands, including Louis Vuitton, Parfums Christian Dior, Jas Hennessy & Co, and Mercier, among others.

Arriving at the Chateau around noon, we were escorted to our rooms and informed that lunch would be served directly after apperitifs, which would be at one pm. This gave me an opportunity to shower and change after the journey, and at the appointed time, a member of the chateau's household knocked on my door. "Sir, I'm here to escort you to lunch." The mists of time have erased the memory of the title of the lady and her daughter, the members of our party from Northern Ireland were introduce to in an ante room to the dining room. But it was very clear both elegant ladies, who were to be our hosts for the weekend, were important members of the Chateau's family.

We enjoyed apperitifs before lunch, and the conversations were easy. Even though it was October, the sun was shining in a clear blue sky, and the temperature mild enough for lunch to be served on a terrace overlooking a vineyard of perfectly rowed vines. The afternoon was spent resting or walking the gardens until dinner that evening, which evolved into a lively affair of beautiful food, wine, and lively conversation and music.

During the rest of the weekend, we visited the Moet et Chandon cellars, some of the vineyards, and continued to enjoy the hospitality of our hosts and good food, wines, champagne and conversation. On Sunday, after lunch, we expressed our appreciation to our hosts, bid farewell, and were driven to Reims Airport, where the corporate jet returned us to Belfast after a memorably and luxurious weekend.

During the rest of 1980 business continued to be extremely healthy, and with my expectation again that year of a very decent bonus, we decided to buy a second house as an investment. Life in Dunadry was good, and work at the inn was both satisfying and financially rewarding. Even though the property was relatively small, I was, at the time, happy to continue my career there indefinitely, so we did the required research and found a small development of pretty two-bedroom bungalows in Balbriggan and decided to purchase one. We planned to rent out the house, but wanted to do so furnished in order to eliminate or minimise any tenant having a long-term claim on its occupancy. Consequently the new house lay empty during much of the winter that year, awaiting the purchase of furniture. About mid-February, I received a frantic call from a neighbour to say that water was pouring out from under the front door. After a quick dash from Dunadry to Balbriggan, Shelley and I entered the house to find the water pipe in the attic had burst and a substantial portion of the ceiling had collapsed. Fortunately, we had insured the house very soon after we'd purchased it, so there was no financial loss, but it did delay our rental plans.

In early March 1981, Brian Faloon, the eldest of the two sons of Paddy Fallon and the one managing the family's farming interests, informed his family that he wished the farms to be sold and the funds received be assigned to him as his share of the family fortune. He planned to move to Australia, where he wanted to purchase an extensive sheep farming business. In due course, Brian's wishes were fulfilled, and he emigrated. Whether Brian's decision precipitated what followed, or was already part of the family's pre-planned strategy, possibly in light of the advancing age of Paddy Faloon, chairman and patriarch of the group, was of course, only known to the family members themselves, who were sole shareholders of all of their companies.

Soon afterwards came the announcement that would eventually impact me: Northern Brick, by far the largest and most profitable of the Faloon enterprises, was being sold to an international company. This considerably reduced the responsibility of Paddy Faloon's managing director, Colin Noble, who would be made redundant.

In spite of my success in turning Dunadry Inn from a permanent loss-maker into a very profitable business, these circumstances now concerned me. It was not just my job and income, but my very comfortable way of life seemed at risk. What if Dunadry Inn was next to be placed on the market? How this would impact my family was of great concern.

Whether there were opportunities locally or whether we would have to move would be of particular consideration for our daughter Erika. By now, she was thirteen years of age and had recently begun her high school education in Antrim Grammar School. In her short school life of eight years to date, she had attended eight schools, and the thought that she might have to again change was a worry for Shelley and I. We had purchased a dog for Erika, a Pekinese. How would a move impact the dog? If we had to give up Smokey, that would only further increase the trauma of moving for Erika. Shelley was very adept at adjusting to any environment, living one day at a time with a special calm and acceptance that was rare. Although the Faloon family asked me to continue managing the hotel, I was concerned, so when Colin Noble approached me with a proposal to seek the purchase of a hotel in North America, I agreed to join him as equal partner. So, I resigned from Dunadry Inn.

Colin and I would continue to work together and combine our efforts in a new endeavour. Colin, as chairman of our new company, would fund a down payment, negotiate with lenders, and eventually manage the finances, external business affairs and expansion of Emerald Hotels, the name we chose for the company. As managing director and general manager, I would manage the hotel operation. We also decided to offer Mima Harper, who was the banquet manager at Dunadry Inn, ten percent of the new company if she would come with us. Mima had been the strongest department head at the inn and would be a definite asset in the new venture. She gladly accepted. Because of the trust that I believed had developed between Noble and myself over the previous four years, and in some way, my naivety, our agreement was verbal at this time and not committed to paper.

The move to North America required me to divest my family of our share of the Westerly sailboat, *Shebe*. Brian Beharrel agreed to buy my half, but he could only do so in monthly payments over the following year. There was a financial burden to this with the loss of interest on the capital plus its immediate unavailability. Also, our next-door neighbour offered to purchase our Dunadry house but did not have any money immediately available. He informed me that funds were on the way to him. This proved false, and we waited for over a year for this transaction to be completed. It never was, and eventually, all the equity in the house in Dunadry was consumed by monthly mortgage payments. We had earlier sold the Balbriggan house to fund the move, so we began anew!

My chef and I with the Mouton Cadet Award at Dunadry Inn

Shelley and I with family and friends at the May Ball in Dunadry
Inn

Shelley and I on New Year's Eve in Dunadry Inn

Chapter Ten

An Hotelier in North America

By April 1981, contacts in both America and Canada were established, travel routes determined, and flight tickets purchased. Colin and I planned to divide between us, the visits to hotels identified as possible acquisitions. However, there were three 'hot' properties we would view together: one in the Florida Keys, the second in Phoenix Arizona, and the third in Sedona, Arizona. These looked, on paper, to have the potential we sought, and the locations were attractive areas in which to begin the quest to develop a multi-property hotel company.

On the appointed date in early April, we flew from Belfast to London, connecting with a transatlantic flight to New York on British Airways. We stayed in New York for a couple of days to gather our bearings and fine-tune the travel plans. On a beautiful early spring morning, we left the hotel in Manhattan for La Guardia Airport and a flight to Miami. A rental car was waiting for us at Miami airport, a large Lincoln Continental. It was more than 150 miles from Miami to Key West, and as we wished to arrive fresh and relaxed, a car that allowed us to journey in comfort provided that assurance. Driving out of the airport and onto the highway, we headed for Florida City, crossed over onto Key Largo, and set off through the several keys and the many bridges we would cross before arriving at our destination.

It was as equally nice a morning as it had been in New York, although warmer and more humid, and of course, the swaying palm trees and the sparkling blue sea confirmed we were now in the tropics. The drive was stunning, and we enjoyed the journey from Key Largo, through Islamorada, and to Long Key, where we stopped for a late lunch. A small restaurant with a wooden deck right on the water overlooking the Gulf of Mexico was ideal and presented an opportunity to have a substantial serving of soft shell crabs, a speciality of Florida. Eaten whole, shell and all, they were delicious, and afterwards, they were washed down by mugs of ice-cold beer. We quickly continued the journey, determined to reach Key West before dark and check into the property we were there to view.

The hotel had one hundred very nicely appointed rooms, a small banquet room, a seafood restaurant, and a bar right on the waterfront boardwalk overlooking the blue waters of the Caribbean Sea. While we had received some revenue figures relating to the business prior to arrival, we were not privy to more extensive information until now. The owner's agent revealed detailed numbers, and afterwards, we toured the property, and the following morning, after a good night's rest, we walked the streets of Key West.

The city is the seat of Monroe County and the southernmost city in the continental United States. It is southwest of Miami, about 160 miles by car, and Cuba, at its closest point, is about ninety miles south. Many Caribbean-bound passenger cruise ships start their voyage from Key West.

While Key West was pretty, the property superb and well maintained, and the business healthy, the numbers, however, would not leave room for further growth, something that Colin and I required. We never met the owner and now did not need to. After the second night, we departed Key West and returned to Miami Airport, disappointed that a property we liked failed to meet our needs.

From Miami, we flew to Phoenix, Arizona, to view the next property on our list, a downtown commercial hotel, where we would meet the owners agent. Leaving Phoenix Airport, we took a taxi to the Camelback Inn in Scottsdale, where we were booked in for two nights. Scottsdale is a vibrant, wealthy city in the eastern part of Maricopa County, adjacent to the greater Phoenix area. The population is estimated to be of about 200,000 living within the city, and the *New York Times* described downtown Scottsdale as "a desert version of Miami's South Beach" and as having "plenty of late night partying and a buzzing hotel scene." Its slogan is 'The West's Most Western Town'. We checked in, Colin phoned the agent, Rick Burton, to let him know we'd arrived and to agree a time to meet the following afternoon.

As we'd just one hotel to view in Phoenix, we decided to take the morning to enjoy the facilities of the world-famous Camelback Inn. It is a stunningly beautiful property of low-rise, desert-coloured, stucco-covered buildings, designed in a typical western style, set in large, well-manicured grounds with swimming pools, a gym, a spa, tennis courts, and several restaurants and bars, all in the shadow of Camelback Mountain.

Rick arrived at the inn around noon, and after an early lunch, we set off to view the hotel in downtown Phoenix. Phoenix is the capital, and largest city, of Arizona, with a population around one and a half million. It has a subtropical desert climate, making it very hot in the summer, with temperatures up to 45C, and cold in the winter, with temperatures frequently below freezing. Being in the centre of the state, it is the jumping off point for the various attractions in the 'Valley of the Sun', as well as the rest of Arizona, and is about halfway between Tucson to the south and Flagstaff to the north. Apart from the mountains surrounding the city, the topography of Phoenix itself is generally flat.

The hotel was another disappointment. It was a high-rise with two hundred rooms in the centre of the city, an excellent location, but it was in an exceptionally rundown condition. It would require huge capital to rehabilitate it to a marketable level, and the potential revenue would not service the investment. We recognised the search would be difficult and we would probably view many properties before we found what we were looking for.

"Colm let's split up, we'll be able to cover more ground quicker," Colin commented after the latest disappointment. I agreed, so we mapped out a plan of action. We had a viewing in Dover Delaware, and Colin checked out of the Camelback Inn and left for the airport and a flight to Dover. Following his departure, Rick came to the inn with details of the viewing in Sedona, so he and I drove there later that same morning. Sedona is several hours from Phoenix, and while the property we viewed there was also a 'no interest', the day spent was a pleasant interlude. Sedona is a very small town in the Arizona desert and represents the Old West as well as a stopping off point to view the red rocks and giant cacti for those on their way to see the Grand Canyon.

Returning to Phoenix, I left the following morning for California to continue the search, viewing hotels in Santiago, Los Angles, and eventually San Francisco, where I found what I believed would fit our requirements. It was a beautiful old one-hundred-bedroom hotel, with a small lobby and space for a small restaurant and bar. It was not operational but had just been completely renovated to a very high standard and was situated right in downtown San Francisco. I believed I could run this property at both a high occupancy and high average room rate and that with the right chef, theme, and marketing strategy, the restaurant could be developed as a unique complement to the hotel, given the location.

During our travels, Colin and I kept in daily contact at a fixed time every evening, and on this occasion when we spoke on the phone, I advised him what I had found. Colin's immediate retort, though, was;

"Colm, get a flight to Winnipeg as quickly as you can. I've found exactly what we need."

Colin's property trumped mine, at least in his mind, so the next morning, I flew to Winnipeg. Early April in Winnipeg is still winter, and upon arriving at one a.m., after a long journey from San Francisco, I surely felt it. Dressed for a California spring rather than a Manitoba winter, I quickly sought the warm interior of a taxi outside the terminal building. With snow on the ground and, the temperature reaching as low as $-30.0°C$, without the windchill, I questioned the logic of living in Winnipeg, the 'Gateway to the West' as the city was refered to. In conversation with the taxi driver as we left the airport, he assured me that although snow sometimes lasts six months of the year, I would enjoy the summers which are warm. For that I would have to wait and see, if I was still here come summer.

The Niakwa Travelodge was the hotel that Colin had found. As it was very late at night, or more precisely, very early morning, and the hotel was on the opposite side of the city, I decided to rely on the taxi driver's local knowledge to find me a hotel near the airport to stay overnight. I was dropped off some ten minutes later at a rather basic motel in a nearby industrial estate and checked-in. Little sleep was awarded me that night, as the several cockroaches in the room, including one or two in the bed, had me spending what was left of the night on a cockroach hunt. This was not a positive introduction to the city of Winnipeg, the province of Manitoba, and the country of Canada: cockroaches, snow, and freezing temperatures. At that moment, San Francisco seemed a far better option.

While the Travelodge needed work on some of its public areas and the guest rooms needing updating, it would be passable for a couple of years. The swimming pool area which was by far the most attractive facility in the hotel was located centrally, surrounded by the bedroom wings. Half of the one hundred and twenty guest rooms either overlooked the pool area or opening directly on to it. The winter sun would shine through it's glass roof onto this indoor tropical paradise, where exotic plants and trees surrounded the substantial pool of shimmering blue water. It was a great place for a 'summer' break during the long and severe Manitoba winters. Families would book into the hotel on weekends for a touch of the tropics, while weekday business consisted mainly of corporate clients.

"What do you think?";

Colin asked me after we toured the property and reviewed the numbers. We agreed it was doing well and had the potential for considerably greater growth.

"Let's go for it";

I said, and the process to acquire what we planned would be the first of many properties in North America began.

While I returned to Northern Ireland to wrap up my affairs and prepare the family for the move to Canada, Colin remained to organise the purchase of the property and negotiate with banks to fund the acquisition. Colin Noble was a very astute and competent negotiator, and against all odds, he acquired the bank funding. The deal was highly leveraged, up to ninety-five percent, but we were confident that additional business was there to be nurtured. And in due course, that confidence proved to be well founded.

Mima Harper continued to work at Dunadry Inn during this period, and it was now time to tell her where we had purchased a hotel and to confirm if she was still interested in joining us. She said "yes absolutely", resigned from Dunadry Inn, and made arrangements to move to Canada.

Smokey, Erika's Pekinese, had grown since he was just a ball of handheld fluff a year earlier and was quite a feisty little mutt. One afternoon, while Shelley and I were packing up in readiness for the move to Canada, we heard Erika shouting from outside. Running out of the house, we saw her chasing Smokey to prevent him from running onto the heavily trafficked road in front of our house. Just in time, Shelley managed to grasp his tail, thus preventing certain death as he darted toward the road, this to the great relief of all. That relief was short lived, however, for the act of saving his life by grabbing his tail damaged his spine and the use of his back legs. He was a sad sight, but as our journey was imminent, we took him to Canada in the hope he would recover. That was not to happen, and in our new home in Winnipeg, within a month, he tumbled down the stairs. With heavy hearts, we had no alternative but to have Smokey put down. While we were all saddened, Erika was particularly distraught.

The newly acquired house in Windsor Park, Winnipeg, had been mortgaged at a numbing twenty-two percent interest. It was the early eighties, and economies were in dire straits.

Erika was enrolled in Windsor Park Junior High School, and we began our new life in Canada. We did have to travel outside the country to collect our 'landed immigrant cards' and the nearest Canadian Consulate was in Minniapolis, so we got in our newly acquired Buick and drove through blinding snow to collect our documents. Throughout the return journey the snow continued but we eventually reached Winnipeg now fully legal as permanent residents.

It was May 1981. There was a sense of urgency about generating new and additional business for the hotel given the huge mortgage we needed to service. We had paid around C$ four and a quarter million for the property, of which C$ four million was leveraged. Along with the hotel, the purchase also consisted of an adjacent commercial building, which housed a bank and a government liquor store, an empty warehouse to its rear and additional parking space. While room revenue was currently at a level we could live with in the short term, it was in the food and beverage areas that the immediate potential for growth existed. The hotel had a cocktail lounge, a coffee shop, and a dining room, and a beverage room. While refurbishing, re-launching, and re-marketing these outlets could generate additional revenue, two areas were identified for maximum growth: the beverage room and the beer off sales outlet.

Manitoba in those days had liquor laws that people from outside the province might consider strange. These strange and archaic rules were changing as the needs of the time demanded. The liquor laws were restrictive, and even unconstitutional in a culture that expected beer, wine, and liquor to be available anywhere people wanted to enjoy it. Up until then, it was illegal in Manitoba to stand up in a bar while drinking. Buying alcohol from a government outlet, which was the only source of wines and liquors, meant filling out a permit with your name and address. And up until 1957, men and women in Manitoba could not share a drink in the same public place. Hotels could obtain a licence to sell alcohol in a 'beverage room', but only if they also had a liquor licence for a dining room, which had to remain open when the beverage room was open so food would be available to the drinkers.

The Travelodge satisfied all the current requirements, and as Emerald Hotels, our company, began taking possession of the property, we dropped Niakwa from the name, and the hotel became the Winnipeg Travelodge. A new sign was erected, and the main entrance to the hotels was redeveloped and redecorated to reflect a new beginning. In the beverage room, which had a sitting capacity of three hundred, we terminated the old Bavarian-style accordion band that generated a couple of thousand dollars sales a week. We redecorated the room, hired the city's top DJs, installed disco-style lighting—and top of the range sounds systems, remember, it was the eighties—applied for one of the new stand-up bar licenses, which was granted, and installed a new stand-up bar, allowing people to stand or move around still holding their drink. It now became a nightclub, which we named Fridays, the hottest in town, and the young people flocked to it. Revenue increased by several thousand percent, with sales of ten to twelve thousand dollars a night, seven nights a week. Even when the room was full, people would continue to line up outside late into the evening, even in the freezing cold, in the hope that someone would leave and they could enter. Fridays was a breathtaking success.

The hotel sold beer by the case from a small retail area at the side of the property, as per the laws of Manitoba. This generated around fifty thousand dollars in sales per month. These sales were mainly six packs, so there was an opportunity for growth here also.

We decided to develop the empty warehouse at the back of the commercial building into a large 'drive through' beer outlet. We installed extra-large coolers and automated delivery systems to drive-up windows and increase the beer range to include twelve and twenty-four bottle cases. It was an instant success. Many Canadians are big beer drinkers, and an almost constant stream of traffic pulled up to the windows for beer. Large groups of young people would come in pickup trucks and load them up with cases of twenty-fours. Revenue jumped to a jaw-dropping million dollars per month. We then renovated the dining room and cocktail lounge, which further enhanced revenues. All this within the first year, and we were now in a good place, a very good place, as business continued to generate substantial revenues into the second year.

The home Shelley and I purchased was about four or five kilometres from the hotel. Colin had a rented townhouse in a complex next door to the hotel while his own family remained in Northern Ireland. Mima Harper was a widow without children and had a townhouse in the same complex as Colin. Without any suggestion of impropriety, Colin and Mima spent considerably more time together than with me and that was fine with me, and indeed understandable. They were alone and I had a family, a wife, a daughter and a home away from the hotel. Over time however, I sensed a widening gap in the relationship between Noble and myself. After a period of a couple of months where food costs were out of alignment, he asked me to move out of my office into a tiny uncomfortable loft above the kitchen, to review what the problem was. It was an unneccessary request that we argued about and which would do nothing to resolve the problem. While this may seem a small thing, but because of the growing gap between us, it resulted in an unpalatable level of tension. At least I felt that, but I'm not sure he did and I knew that all was not right, for as yet, no shares had been assigned to me. Consequently I had no leverage to resist.

Noble had continuously deflected any discussion about the division of shareholdings in the company during the first couple of years of operation. In my trusting nature, and indeed, some degree of naivety, I reluctantly accepted his argument, that we should stay focused on growing the business. This, I later recognised, as a rather hollow explanation about delays in drawing up share holder agreements, or issuing share certificates. This delay in addressing the subject further increased tension. Was this part of some plan? Emerald Hotels owned the Travelodge, but who owned Emerald Hotels? I didn't, for I had no equity, yet the company was a legally registered entity.

By the end of the second year, the relationship between Noble and I had deteriorated to an untenable level. I trustingly sought advice from someone I knew and thought was trustworthy. That conversation was shared with Noble, who claimed I was disloyal and used this as the basis to force me from the company.

In actuality, since I never was party to a shareholder agreement, I was just an employee and was sacked with a redundancy payment of a paultry five thousand dollars. In retrospect, I believed this might have been the plan all along. Having me as general manager after the success of Dunadry Inn would contribute positively to the Winnipeg Travelodge. It did!

It was a devastating blow, and over several years that followed, the loss of my dreams of being a partner in my own hotel, and eventually, a multi hotel company was difficult to deal with.

Years later., I learned that Noble did go on to be very successful, with his company owning or managing dozens of hotels in America.

The loss of that goal was more devasting to me than the financial loss, then about three million dollars in mortgaged equity. My strenght of will, my character, and time itself, about four or five years, overcame the pain and the anquish and this chapter eventually faded into irrelevance in my life. And indeed Shelley's support, understanding and ability to accept whatever transpired with a calmness which was always not just helpful, but inspiring. She was our family's rock.

We decided we should seek legal advice. We were introduced to a lawyer in one of the top legal firms in Winnipeg. He agreed to work on developing a suit against Emerald Hotels for wrongful termination of employment and the recovery of my forty-five percent equity share value.

Following several weeks' work on the case, one Monday morning, we were scheduled to meet with Emerald Hotels and presumably, their lawyers, when I received a phone call from our law firm. The call conveyed terrible news that intensefied the stress we were already under. The caller advised me that my lawyer had suffered a fatal heart attack that weekend. The firm was closed for the funeral and a three-day mourning period. Furthermore, I was advised that it would take several months for the files to be reconstructed and allocated to other members of the firm, as much of the strategy might have been committed to their departed lawyer's memory and not yet to paper. By this time, I was quite despondent and unable to handle the situation any further. I was ready to move on to whatever other opportunity might present itself, and accepted the five thousand dollars from Emerald Hotels.

During this difficult period, Ray Weldon, who was a regular

customer of the Travelodge, wanted me to partner with him in a hotel venture in Ontario and had approached me on several occasions. Following my separation from Emerald Hotels, I accepted the offer, admittedly without a great deal of thought and somewhat out of desperation. I now had no compunction about hiring staff from the Travelodge; they had stolen my future. I offered the chef and two bar managers jobs in the Bala Bay Inn in Muskoka, Ontario.

The Bala Bay Inn was the hotel that Ray Weldon had purchased and I would manage as an equal partner. The hotel, a small one, had been closed for a couple of years after the previous owners had gone bankrupt following the renovation of all thirty-four bedrooms, which were still in new condition. They'd also renovated much of the public areas, which consisted of a small pub, a cocktail lounge, and a restaurant. The property was located directly on Lake Muskoka and had a small dock on the lake for visiting boaters.

It was early spring of 1983, and I needed the hotel to open for the summer season of that year, so my three managers and I set about preparing to leave Winnipeg for Bala a small village just outside the town of Gravenhurst in the Muskoka region of Ontario, about eighty kilometres north of Toronto. We rented a U-Haul truck, loaded it up with our personal belongings, headed onto the Trans-Canada Highway, and set out on the two-thousand-kilometre journey to our destination. We drove from dawn until late night, passing by Kenora, Thunder Bay, North Bay, and Gravenhurst eventually arriving in Bala. The journey took us an exhausting three days, and we were happy it was over.

I sent for Shelley and Erika soon afterwards. We left Winnipeg without the possibility of selling our house in such a short time, or from a distance of two thousand kilometres, so with little equity in the property and no way of funding the high interest rates, we handed the keys back to the bank that held the mortgage.

With a short pre-opening period before the season began, there was little time for external marketing, and that summer of 1983, the hotel relied almost solely on 'walk in' trade. But some of that trade turned out to be less than desirable. The Bala Bay Dance Hall across from the inn was open nightly during the short summer and was a regular hangout for biker gangs, their women, and their groupies, who made Bala their summer destination. Unexpectedly, they were the walk-in trade for the Bala Bay Inn, and many party nights in the rooms required the hotel staff to constantly request quiet and, on more than one occasion, required the intervention of the police.

While Erika was again in a new school at Gravenhurst, her experience in changing schools may have honed her ability to make friends, as it appeared she easily did so, and this time at least, the change in school seemed less traumatic. The summer quickly passed, and the 'party' crowd departed Bala, soon to be supplanted by the more sedate traditional guests, up to Muskoka for the fall season and the magnificent autumn colours of golds, yellows, and reds of varying hues. Fall gave way to winter, the snowflakes began to fall, and Bala was left to the locals, and the Royal Canadian Legion hall for dances on a Saturday night.

It was a somewhat bleak time of the year, but the Bala Bay Inn had survived its first season under my management, albeit a difficult one. It had not made a profit but had attained an operating breakeven point. This, however, did not satisfy Ray Weldon, who felt that there should have been a surplus to expenses. Weldon had been a farmer in Yorkshire in the north of England. He'd sold his farm and came to Canada to purchase a business, and decided the hotel business was the one he wanted to be involved in. He had no experience in the hospitality industry and had demonstrated unreasonable expectations throughout the short period we owned Bala Bay Inn. There were constant heated discussions between him and I, and the relationship between us was souring just as quickly as the winter snows began to fall. We agreed to part company that fall of 1983. Weldon put the hotel on the market and used the equity to leverage an animal feed business he purchased locally. This seemed a more appropriate venture, given his background.

I was now on unemployment insurance, which would sustain us until it ran out in nine months or I found a job. Not unlike failed marriages, I had two failed partnerships and now the lesson learned, that maybe I was not partnership compatible. The winter months passed slowly. I submitted hundreds of job applications and answered dozens of job ads in the newspapers, but nothing was forthcoming. I was soon to be forty-two years of age, with a wife, a daughter, penniless, and nothing to show for my years.

Come the spring of 1984, my unemployment insurance was almost exhausted. Once gone, my family would have to go on welfare and we would have to vacate the house we lived in, for we would not be able to afford the rent. I could feel I was once more sinking deeper and deeper into a black hole from which I might be unable to ascend, and all the time the experience in Winnipeg continued to haunt me. To be swallowed up by the dark raging river that snaked its way past the rear of our garden in Bala on those bleak days began to draw me in. It looked a tempting way to end the despair that burdened me, but fear of eternal damnation and the legacy of poverty I would leave my family, precipitated second thoughts. I was desperate to find a way out of the fog of doom and gloom, when I heard of a five-day residential program in Toronto run by an Anglian church minister, designed to help executives who had lost their jobs or business interests.

This period in the early eighties was one when the corporate mantra was 'flatten the organisation, increase productivity, and cull the workforce.' As a consequence, there were many valuable, experienced managers and executives who suddenly found themselves on dole lines. All this took a toll on their self-esteem, self-worth, and of course, their pockets. Pastor John (not his real name), who ran a parish in the financial district of Toronto, knew many of these individuals personally and wanted to help, so he set about developing, organising, and marketing a program which he very appropriately titled "Boot-Straps", 'Lift yourself up by your bootstraps' being the obvious implication. I signed up, for I had nothing else to do and on the appointed Sunday evening, I drove my big Buick from Bala to Toronto and checked in to the retreat house where the program was being held over the next five days. My hope was that it would help me deal with the disappointments and stress of the past few years.

There were about thirty participants in the program, all were previously managers, directors, and executives from a variety of industries, and as I met them, it helped knowing there were others in situations similar to mine. Since John was a pastor, it was not unexpected that there would be some religious component. In fact, there was not, other than to use the analogy of Christ's crucifixion, death, and resurrection to represent the participants' dismissal, subsequent despair at the death of their careers, and, through Boot Straps, their eventual resurrection. This was the core of the program, and through group and individual activities, along with introspection, one learned to deal with dismissal and subsequent despair and at the end of that week, feel resurrected from the all-pervasive gloom, recognising this is just life.

The final Friday afternoon, as I retrieved my car for the drive back to Bala, I felt an overwhelming sense of gratitude and contentment. It was a strange feeling of lightness, as if a great weight had been lifted from me. On the drive home, I stopped to buy Shelley a rose as a gesture of appreciation for her unwavering encouragement and support. She never expressed one word of doubt in my ability to get past our dark times, never one word of negativity, or one indication of discontent. This gift of a rose may seem a small thing, but I was not very demonstrative, and giving flowers to her was, regrettably, a rare event. I loved her more than

I could say and wished I could express more completely what was in my heart, but words of emotion always failed me. I was pragmatic, calculating, unemotional and I recognized these characteristics in myself, which may, or may not, have been the consequence of something from my formative years.

With renewed spirit, I returned to the job search and soon answered an advertisement in *The Globe and Mail* for a training advisor for the hotel school of Bermuda College. This was a dream job on a beautiful semi-tropical island and would be a perfect new start, if I was granted an interview and selected. Within a relatively short period of time, I received a letter from Bermuda College inviting me for an interview in a Toronto hotel. I met Roger Regimbal, the hotel school's director, and Dan Marshall, the head of training. I felt the interview went well, but was advised that were three hundred applicants. While not all applicants were interviewed, there was a significant number that were, and it would take a few weeks for a candidate to be selected. I returned to Bala feeling hopeful.

With only one payday left on my unemployment insurance and, consequently, one step away from welfare, the situation was bleak. However, within a couple of weeks of the interview, I received a letter from the Hotel School of Bermuda College at Stonington Beach offering me the position of training advisor to the Bermuda hotel industry under the auspices of Bermuda College.

With a generous tax-free salary and living allowance, I felt truly 'resurrected'. I had survived the storms of two acrimoniously failed partnerships and had the financial scars to show for it. I was penniless but positive about the future, and of course, I accepted the offer unreservedly in my return reply.

Shelley and I held an auction in our front garden to sell off our furniture, household goods and the car, the big Buick, in order to raise some much needed cash for we had none. We took our collection of paintings, artwork, curios, oriental carpets, and any personal items we could not take to Bermuda to a self-storage locker in Toronto. We would not part with those items that reflected our life up untill then. They were all that was left of our possessions. We would travel to Bermuda with only our personal clothing and, oddly, our cutlery, bed linens and towels. Anything else we chose to bring would be dutiable and for our personal account.

The one dark spot was Erika changing schools again. How she ever received an education at all is a mystery. Ten or twelve schools in a child's life is staggering. Whether she complained or not then, is lost to a foggy memory, but one could imagine she might have.

That spring of 1984, we left Bala Bay, Ontario, Canada for Bermuda.

Shelley and I at Bala Bay Inn

Travelodge Winnipeg, Manitoba, Canada

Chapter Eleven
Bermuda

Surrounded by an azure blue sea, with contrasting pink sand beaches, perfectly manicured, clean, green, and pristine undulating landscapes dotted with snow-white-roofed homes painted in pastel shades of pinks and blues and greens, with a predominance of pink, this is Bermuda. It is a fantasy island approximately twenty miles in length and two miles wide, set in the Atlantic Ocean seven hundred miles east of the North Carolina coast, with a population of approximately fifty-thousand. Bermuda's sub-tropical climate has hot, humid summers cooled by frequent showers that replenish the island's water supply. There are no rivers in Bermuda, yet their water management system is so efficient that they can maintain several world-class golf courses. This all supports a vibrant tourist industry. Bermuda's white roofs serve a practical as well as decorative purpose: the lime they are painted with helps purify the rainwater that flows from the roofs into the large sumps under every home.

Having arrived in Bermuda bereft of all but a few dollars in cash and with a balance of nine hundred dollars on my credit card, one of my earlier requests of the college was to support my application to the bank for a loan to purchase a car and a moped. This was readily granted, and a small second-hand Honda and a moped were soon acquired. Due to the very narrow roads, cars are limited to one per household, with an engine capacity not more than 1,300CC, and mopeds and scooters are a common form of transportation. Both vehicles were in excellent condition, assured by the system in Bermuda where cars were subjected to rigid government inspection each year, not just for safety and reliability, but also for body condition. A small dent or a scratch would fail the vehicle inspection, requiring the owner to repair it and return for re-inspection. If the car was in a generally unsatisfactory condition, it could be confiscated and crushed, thus ensuring pristine cars complemented the pristine houses and gardens throughout the island.

Bermuda was to be our home for the forseeable future. Erika would finish school here, finally completing her fractured education in preparation for university. Shelley would also work in order to help rebuild the family's finances.

Arriving at Bermuda Airport, located on a small American military base, in the darkness of a late spring night, we were met by a representative of the college and driven to our new home, a tiny cottage near the hotel school. We had flown from Toronto to New York to Bermuda. Tired and unprepared for what greeted us on the walk from the gate to the front door of our new home, we encountered dozens of very large frogs or toads that littered the front garden and the walkway while loudly croaking their welcome. Stepping gingerly over the knot of toads, we entered the rather sparsely furnished cottage. We had been advised to bring only bed and bath linens and cutlery, as anything else would be dutiable. The bed linen was quickly hauled out of the suitcase, the beds were made up, and we 'crashed' for the night.

The next morning, Dan Marshall, the training director, arrived at the cottage to collect me and take me to the hotel school, which was located in beautiful gardens on the edge of Stonington beach. "Welcome to Bermuda and Bermuda College, Colm," was Rogers Regimbal, the school director's immediate and friendly greeting.

"Dan, why don't you take Colm on a tour of the school and hotel."

The Stonington Beach hotel had sixty guest rooms, a full-service dining room, a cocktail lounge, and a small banquet room. Although small compared to schools like Cornell, it was well equipped, and like Cornell's Statler Inn, where students received hands-on practice, Stonington also had the Stonington Beach Hotel, where students trained. Following the tour, I was taken to the training office, shown to my desk, and given my mandate: "Training for quality service in the Bermuda Hotel industry!" If there were goals, objectives, or a strategy to achieve this, that was undisclosed and, for the moment, a mystery. How I was to do this, it seemed, I had to figure out for myself.

Meanwhile, Shelley began organising our home and purchasing food and household supplies. There was a small supermarket nearby, and she and Erika shopped there after spending part of the day exploring the new neighbourhood. We eventually settled into a routine, with Erika off to school at Bermuda College and Shelley working in a restaurant in Hamilton, the capital of Bermuda.

Hospitality companies began to recognise that one of the most important keys to success in the early eighties was quality. Competition was keen in all services industries, particularly in the hotel industry, where takeovers, mergers, upsizing, downsizing, and consolidations were becoming common. Quality Circles were the new management tools to improve productivity and quality, where groups of employees would meet on a regular basis and be trained to identify, analyse, and recommend to management the implementation of solutions to the problems which impacted their own work area. Many organisations acknowledged that those who did the work most often understood better the problems inhibiting performance.

It was agreed by the college that Dan Marshal and I should attend the Quality Circle Institute in Chico, California, to learn the techniques used in quality circles. Upon our return to Bermuda, the hotel school invited all general managers of the Bermuda hotels to a presentation on quality circles given by Dan and I. While general managers and their executive committees would be the cheerleaders of the process, department managers and supervisors would be the implementers, permitting meetings of their employees to take place during working hours, allowing them to identify problems, and listening to their solutions. Middle managers were sometimes insecure about allowing employees to have that much authority. They feared the loss of power and that their jobs might be in jeopardy: if their employees could solve all the problems were they needed? It was essential to reassure them of the value of the process and that senior management would support them.

The process was greeted with enthusiasm at the presentation, and immediately, two hotels offered their properties to pilot Bermuda's first quality circles. I would manage the implementation in one hotel, and Dan in the other. The general managers selected the departments where the first circles were to be tested, one department in each of the two hotels. These were well-managed departments where success was more likely to be achieved, which would, in turn, encourage others to sign on to the process.

While this was the focus of my work, it was not so demanding that personal time was unavailable. Unlike hotel operation, where, frequently, a manager's availability may be required at any time of the day or night, I worked a nine-to-five day with weekends off, a rare privilege for an hotelier. I purchased a North Star twenty-nine-foot sailboat named *Ebony* and a mooring near Darrel's Wharf in Hamilton Harbour. We were happy to be back on the water again after a number of years away from the coast in Canada and many weekends were spent sailing *Ebony* in the Great Sound or out of the Sound and down to St George, Bermuda's second town at the end of the island.

Life took on a comfortable routine, with work relaxed and ordered and free time enjoyed. Shelley and I made friends with two other couples, Canadians Sue and Stu, and British Philipa and Bill, and we spent much of our free time together. On weekends, when we were not sailing, we went to Horseshoe Bay, Bermuda's most popular beach. The Hamilton Princess was a favourite location for Sunday brunch. On other occasions, we would lunch at the White Heron Inn, where simple but tasty food was served and the young expatriate crowd would hang out, drinking beer, swimming in the pool, or listening to Neil, the resident entertainer, on voice and guitar.

The lifestyle was easy, relaxed, comfortable and devoid of stress and I began to recover from the trauma of my two failed partnerships. While the mental weight of what happened in Canada would remain for a while longer, life in Bermuda helped ease the pain.

In the spring of 1985, Erika graduated from Bermuda College, and as the opportunity for work or further education on the Island was limited, after much discussion and soul searching, it was decided that she should go to Dublin to live with her grandparents, where she could investigate what study or work opportunities might be available in Ireland. My parents were happy to have their oldest grandchild, and the flat they had at the top of their house was hers for the duration. Eventually, she enrolled in a secretarial course in Dublin. During this time, she applied for university entrance to several universities in Ireland and Great Britain and also to the University of Winnipeg, where she was accepted. In the summer of 1986, she returned to Bermuda, and just before term time, she and I flew to Winnipeg to get her settled into the university. I returned to Bermuda, and Erika stayed in her friend Wanda's parents' house until she and Wanda could find a flat together.

Soon after Erika began her studies in Winnipeg University, my father, passed away. He had a heart condition for several years and although it did not impede him from enjoying life, it eventually lead to his death. We had not seen him for a few years and my understanding was that he died in hospital and suffered little. I immediately left on a flight for New York for a connecting flight to Dublin; my younger sister Sedra, who lived in New York at the time, joined me on the same flight. At his funeral I did not view the body as others did, nor did I view my mother's body when she died many years later. While I loved my father, I didn't feel close to him, and as was in character, I took a pragmatic rather than emotional view of his passing.

Death is part of life!

Erika was upset that she was unable to attend the funeral because of university. Following the first semester, she called to say Winnipeg University was not for her. Possibly the distance from her family, the loss of her grandfather whom she had recently lived with, and her inability to attend his funeral were all too much for her, so she returned to Bermuda. A solution was essential for Erika's future, so she decided she would go to London and stay with her friend Candy. There was every expectation that in London, she would find work, and she did.

In spite of our best efforts, our constant support, and training in hotels with quality circles, by 1986, the process was failing. The essential support required from senior management had faded as they'd slipped back into their old ways. The common excuses cited were "lack of time" or "we're too busy", and there were several other excuses not to try a new way of managing. It was both exasperating and disheartening, we felt we somehow owned that failure. What could we have done differently? No answer was forthcoming. We abandoned the process, and I took on classroom work.

The course I taught to final-year students was Quality Assurance, a broad-brush course I developed using some material from the quality circle process, such as problem identification, root cause and effect analysis, and solution development, along with group dynamics to ensure teamwork. I also had instructor diplomas in organization and administration and food and beverage purchasing from Michigan State University, and these subjects were added to the curriculum for third-year management students. And I developed a simple geography program for the students who were on a one-year front office course. After graduation, when working at the front desk in a hotel, they would be confident in the knowledge they understood where their guests came from and could converse with them about their home country, city, or culture. About ten hours of classroom time a week required about twenty-five hours of prep, so I now had about a thirty-five hour week in my new role, and so my relationship with the Hotel School of Bermuda College continued.

Erika departed Bermuda for London, and she would never again live at home. Shelley and I returned to our daily routine, me at the college and Shelley at Longtail restaurant in Hamilton. On weekends, it was either sailing, beaching, brunching, or lunching. Life continued relaxed, lazy, and easy!

It was September 25, 1987, when the fury of Hurricane Emily rained down upon Bermuda, leaving a trail of destruction estimated to be in the millions of dollars. Hundreds of homes and many hotels succumbed to her anger, their roofs torn off, their windows shattered, and their gardens and amenities destroyed. Pleasure boats and yachts were lifted like toys onto the shore. Power was lost, and in many places, including where Shelley and I lived, normalcy would not be restored for weeks. Trees toppled by the hurricane littered the streets, severely limiting the movement of traffic. Bermuda was at a standstill.

As the sky darkened, Hurricane Emily arrived at seven thirty a.m. and the eye passed over the island at nine a.m. It was a very fast-moving hurricane, and we had been aware of its pending arrival from radio news warnings. For us, it began with the rattling of the front door to our house, and as the vibrations increased in speed and intensity, we feared the loud drumming door would not hold and might implode into the living room. I hastily secured one of my neckties from the inside handle of the front door to a hall closet handle and prayed it would not give way. I had no rope, but it held. As the roar of the hurricane rose to deafening decibels and Emily's anger increased, we stood under the lintel of an inside doorway, the safest place in a house during a hurricane. The house shook, and the windows rattled, threatening to cave in to this terrifying force of nature.

It lasted a little over an hour, and suddenly, there was a deathly silent stillness and an eerie, slightly orange-grey glow in the air and sky, as the eye passed over Bermuda. We went outside to review any damage. The external wall of the house was completely covered with leaves, as if an invisible hand had pasted them on. The house, a solid stone structure, fortunately, sustained no damage other than a roof tile imbedded in the front wall. Our next-door neighbour was not quite so fortunate. He had a garage under his living room, and with it's door caved in, the wooden floor of his living room vibrated violently up and down, sending furniture to one end of the room, with most of it beyond repair.

The quiet died, and the wind and noise slowly resumed—the eye had passed, and the opposite side of the hurricane was moving towards us. We quickly returned inside the house to await it's passing. The violence began again, but by about ten thirty a.m. the sky brightened, and it was over. The powerful, hurricane had left Bermuda decimated, and its trail of destruction would take weeks to clear and cost millions of dollars.

Our house was on a hill in Paget Parish, and there were no trees on our road, but on Middle Road, the main thoroughfare out of our residential complex, as on many other roads throughout the island, there were downed trees, poles, and power lines everywhere. Yachts had broken their moorings and been thrown on shore as if they were toys. A large cruise ship that had been tied up alongside Front Street in Hamilton had pulled the mooring bollards out of the ground and drifted into the sound. The crew had managed to get the engines started and been able to hold it against the hurricane to avoid running aground. Electricity was out for about a week; therefore, the pump that pumped water from the water storage sump under the house was inoperable, so I had to regularly climb down into the tank with bucket in tow for water.

With great assistance from other countries and a herculean effort from Bermuda authorities, normal life eventually resumed. Three or four months passed, and one morning, I received a letter from the Canadian Immigration Authorities. They advised me that since we had not lived in Canada for more than three years, our landed immigrant status would not be renewed unless we returned to Canada or purchased a home there within a reasonable timeframe.

We were not yet Canadian citizens, and our landed immigrant status, which was renewed annually, was important for us to eventually become citizens. Bermuda College had recently dissolved the position of training advisor, making me redundant, so in January 1988, we left Bermuda and returned to Toronto, Canada.

My mother Betty, myself, Erika, Shelley, and friend Stuart in Bermuda

Erika and I at Horseshoe Bay, Bermuda

Sailing *Ebony* with, Shelley, and friends off Bermuda

Chapter Twelve
Nova Scotia, Canada

Sue and Stu Miller Nichol, our friends from Bermuda, had departed the island the previous year and now lived in Thornhill, a suburb north of Toronto. They invited us to stay with them for as long as we wished.

I now had to begin the process of finding work. Our time in Bermuda had greatly restored our financial health. Now it was important to take the time to make the right choices in employment something I had not always done in the past. After several weeks with the Miller Nichols, we felt we could impose upon our friends' generosity no longer and decided to move into a service apartment in downtown Toronto, where I could focus greater attention on seeking work. I threw a 'wide net', as the quality of the job was of greater importance than its location. While we were willing to move anywhere in Canada, a move to Vancouver was preferential. The relevant department of the United Nations had for six consecutive years designated Vancouver "the best city in the world in which to live". We decided to organise the move, purchase a car, rent a trailer, and plan the journey. The job search, in the meantime, continued.

Prior to our departure for Bermuda almost four years earlier, we had rented a small self-storage unit in the Toronto area to store those personal effects we had kept following the auction in Bala of most of our other belongings. The only furniture was the brass table Shelley's kindergarten class had given her as a wedding present some twenty years earlier. The rest was our collection of paintings, art pieces, curios, china, books, silverware, carpets, photo albums and other bits and pieces. It was now time to check the storage unit. From the warehouse reception, we proceeded with one of the staff to our unit, opening it up, to our horror we found it empty, nothing, everything we owned gone, all our memories of the past two decades missing.

Extremely upset, I demanded answers.

"My God! Where's our stuff? I barked.

The question was received with an open-mouthed, blank expression on the face of the employee. It was apparent that it was equally as much a surprise to him. Returning to the reception fuming with anger, the manager assured me they would immediately investigate. Eventually, we learned that during our time in Bermuda, ownership of the business had changed, a fact that should have been communicated to all customers. This had not happened, at least not to us. Following the change in ownership, our unit had been flooded, and our property moved to an alternative locker. After much searching the new locker was located and we found all was in order, with no water damage, a huge relief. We renewed rental of the locker until we decided where we would eventually be living.

A few days prior to our move to Vancouver, I received a response to my application to ITT Sheraton Hotel Corporation. The letter was from Ms. Nan Palmer, regional director of human resources, North America Division. She asked me to phone her which I immediately did.

"Hello Ms. Palmer, this is Colm Madden, I'm calling in response to your letter."

"Good morning Mr. Madden, thank you for calling. We're very impressed with your resume and would like to consider you for a position"

"That would be great, thank you" "

"It's as director of training for our Hotel in Halifax, Nova Scotia. Do you know Nova Scotia Colm"

"No I don't Ms Palmer, but to work with Sheraton I'm happy to go wherever I'm sent"

"Execellent, it is subject, of course, to several interviews. Could you travel to New York to meet with me."?

"Absolutely, when would you like me to come"?

"As soon as you can, and you'll also need to continue to Boston to our head office to meet with Jim Smith, our corporate vice president of human resources, and finally to Nova Scotia to meet with the hotel general manager, Hugh Harper. So Colm book flights, let me know the timings and we'll organize our schedules accordingly".

"Okay, I'll get on that once we're off the phone and call you back"

"Excellent, Good bye for now"

"G' bye Ms. Palmer".

Early the following morning, I flew from Toronto's Pearson Airport to New York, and then took a taxi into Manhattan to the New York Sheraton Hotel, where the regional office for the North American division was located and where I was to meet with Nan Palmer. Upon my arrival at the hotel, I was advised to call home as my wife had phoned with an urgent message.

"Colm, I've had three phone calls since you left this morning, one from the Hilton Hotel in Hamilton, Ontario, one from a First Nations Reservation in Ontario, where they have a hotel school, and one from a restaurant chain in Vancouver. All were interested in speaking with you about a position."

I decided not to return the calls until the current round of interviews with Sheraton were completed. My meeting with Nan Palmer seemed successful. After lunch, I returned to the airport to continue on to Boston, where the world headquarters of ITT

Sheraton was located, and my meeting with Jim Smith. I received a positive commitment from both Palmer and Smith, and the position was mine, subject to the agreement of the hotel general manager in Halifax, Nova Scotia. Arriving at Halifax Airport, I took a taxi for the thirty-minute journey into the city centre and the Sheraton Hotel. It was late, almost midnight, and I was hungry and exhausted and was not expecting to meet the general manager that evening. As I checked in, I was handed a note from Hugh Harper suggesting that I should have a good night's rest and we could meet in the morning whenever I was ready—a suggestion I gladly accepted!

Next morning, I arose early, had a quick breakfast and set out to explore this pretty city and I was impressed with what it had to offer. I climbed the pathway up Citedel Hill an elevated park with a military fort at it's centre, located right in the middle of the city. From there, I had the most fantastic three hundred and sixty degree view of the city, the harbour, Bedford Basin and the Atlantic Ocean, just as the sun was rising over the sea's horizon in the east. Although my original idea was to go to the West Coast upon my return from Bermuda, a senior position in this beautiful hotel right on the waterfront of a spectacular natural harbour in this lovely little city would be a very agreeable alternative.

I met with Hugh Harper at eleven a.m. for a discussion on what I could offer to benefit the hotel. This was followed by lunch, and during dessert and coffee, Harper said;

"Colm, we'd like you to join us here at the Halifax Hotel as director of training."

I now had to decide between a firm offer from Sheraton or pursue the interest from Hilton Hotels, the First Nation's Hotel School in Ontario, or the restaurant chain in Vancouver. When it rains, it pours!

"That's fantastic Mr Harper, I really appreciate the offer. But if it's okay with you, can I just have a couple of days to think about it."

"Of course," was the immediate response.

Following my return to Toronto that same evening, Shelley and I set about evaluated the choices before us and eventually decided I would join the Sheraton Halifax Hotel in Nova Scotia. It was a decision I would never regret.

Moving to Halifax, we purchased an apartment on the other side of the harbour in Dartmouth, and a Bayfield 23 sailboat and I joined the Dartmouth Yacht Club. As I settled into my new position, Shelley obtained a job with the Nova Scotia Hilton hotel as front office receptionist, and over the next few years, Erika came to visit us from London, as did my sister Sedra and her family from New York and my mother from Dublin.

Within a year, Hugh Harper was transferred to the Sheraton Hotel in Nashville, Tennessee, and the human resources director, who was American, was transferred back to a US property.

I was promoted to director of human resources, and a new general manager, Bernd Locke, was appointed. He was formerly regional director in the Far East and general manager of the Hong Kong Sheraton, a very large hotel in that iconic city. It seemed a strange move to a relatively small Canadian city and a three-hundred-room hotel! As management staff became aware of these facts, many speculated that something was amiss. And indeed, it was! The position of director of food and beverage had also been recently vacated, and Locke brought along a former food and beverage director with whom he had worked in the Middle East: Charles X, we'll call him. Locke and Charles soon acquired the nicknames among the staff of Yogi Bear and Booboo because they walked around the hotel everywhere together, usually with Booboo in tandem with Yogi Bear. Often, these tours excluded managers even within their own departments. During the many months that followed the appointment of these two individuals, the relationship between them and the rest of the staff, both management and employees, became increasingly more tenuous as they both exhibited similar rather strange traits.

In parallel, my reputation grew exponentially, and I became highly regarded at the corporate level. I was involved in the development of several corporate programs for enhancing the skills of the company's directors, managers, and supervisors and would regularly travel to New York as a member of the development team. There, I would often meet Nan Palmer and, on some occasions, Jim Smith, corporate vice president of human resources, and my personal relationship with them grew. My views, ideas, and suggestions were listened to, and it appeared that Bernd Locke was either aware of that, or had some idea that might be the case. He would frequently visit me in my office and sit and chat in a somewhat subdued manner, something completely out of character when dealing with other staff. I often felt these conversations were intended to elicit some perceived useful inside information I might have possessed. Locke's treatment of staff bordered on abuse, fuelled by a substantial dose of self-righteous narcasistic arrogance. In any event, I'd been 'through the wars' in my life and was not easily intimidated.

One day, while walking through the executive offices, I decided to test the mood of the day and see what Charles X was up to. I stepped into Charles's office and was confronted by a strange and most offensive sight, a large leather bullwhip hanging on the wall behind Charles's desk with a sign below proclaiming "EMPLOYEE INCENTIVE PLAN".

"What's the idea of that? Come on Charles take that thing down. Has any of the staff been in your office and seen it".

"No".

"Good, then please remove it before anyone sees it"

I told him as I left his office.

This was the most blatant example of what Sheraton, as a company, was not. Its reputation as an employer with very positive employee relations was well known. As director of human resources, it was my responsibility to ensure that a work environment in line with the company's philosophy of supporting and training employees for exceptional customer service was upheld. Happy employees lead to happy customers was a fundamental pillar of the way the company operated. This was frequently supported by the fact that the employees rejected the constant advances of the trade unions, of which there were several. With the help of the company's labour relations lawyers, I had strategies in place to reinforce the wishes of both the employees and the company to reject trade unionism.

Soon after the incident with Charles, it was Bernd Locke's turn to demonstrate his own oddity. David McGill was the front office manager and owned a Jeep Cherokee, a rugged four-wheel drive vehicle suitable for all weather conditions and off-road driving. It was entirely appropriate for Canada, especially in winter. Upon his arrival in Nova Scotia, Locke decided he would buy a Jeep Cherokee. His, though, had to be better than McGill's since he was general manager and McGill only front office manager, so he loaded it with every possible extra. Soon after this acquisition, he invited David McGill down to the underground parking lot of the hotel to view his new jeep. Driving around the city, he insisted that McGill agree that Locke's jeep was better than his own, while telling him that the watch he was wearing cost as much as David made in a year.

The strange, arrogant, and abusive incidents continued over the next year. They are too many and too odd to list, but suffice is to say that each incident led us deeper into the abyss of 'black management'. Eventually, the behaviour of both Locke and X had deteriorated to a point where I decided I needed to involve corporate, as no amount of subtle, or indeed overt commentary from me had succeeded in improving the situation. Given Locke's long tenure with the company, his earlier seniority, and his reputed personal friendship with Sheraton's CEO, John Kapiotas, it was a risk, but counting on my good standing with corporate, I informed Nan Palmer regional director of human resources of the behaviours, and the 'ball was now in her court'. Very shortly thereafter, Bernd Locke went on vacation to Toronto for two weeks. He never returned to the Halifax Sheraton Hotel.

I later learned Locke mistakenly believed that his friendship with John Kapioltas was his security. He was seriously mistaken. While in Toronto, he was asked to meet with the company's legal counsel from Corporate in Boston, resulting in Bernd Locke's retirement from Sheraton Hotels. In Halifax, with the agreement of the corporate human resources office, I asked Charles X for his resignation, which was immediately forthcoming without argument or discussion. Undoubtedly, Charles saw the writing on the wall after Locke failed to return from vacation, and he would probably have known from Locke himself what had transpired.

Shortly afterwards Nan Palmer shared with me the mystery of Locke's transfer from Hong Kong to Halifax. There were several serious complaints in Hong Kong from female staff about his behaviour, which subsequently led to his move. This move needed to be as distant as possible. And from Hong Kong to Halifax was about as distant as one could get.

Sheldon Suga was appointed general manager of the Halifax Sheraton shortly afterwards and was a breath of fresh air.

The year that followed Sheldon's appointment was one of calm routine, the kind of easiness within which I would feel the grey clouds of boredom starting to settle over me. My thirty-year career to date had been frenetic, which would have shaped who I now was, a kind of minor-adventure junkie, at least within the framework of my own work experience and possibly even within my life in totality. For in the hospitality industry, the lines between work, play, and private life is often blurred. Work is life and life is work. I needed to constantly find new challenges in new places, with new people and new cultures. I longed for a new horizon and was determined to approach corporate to seek a change. My staff was well capable of ensuring continuity of the culture of the organisation. Before I could approach Nan Palmer, though, I received a call from her. It was the early summer of 1991.

"Colm, next month, when you're in New York for the leadership meeting, please meet with me. I have an opportunity I'd like to discuss with you."

"Okay Nan I'll do that. Anything I should know in advance?" I asked, curious to find out what was it about.

 "No Colm, we'll chat when we meet"

The meeting took place with Nan, in June 1991, and she presented me with a hugely exciting transfer opportunity. I accepted the offer without a moment's hesitation, and in October 1991, Shelley and I were on a flight to Miami, with an onward connection to the island of St. Maarten in the Caribbean and my new position.

With Sheraton Hotel Halifax, Nova Scotia, colleagues

Me sailing in Halifax Harbour, with the Sheraton Hotel in the background

Chapter Thirteen

St Maarten and the Caribbean Casino

The French *Saint Martin* and the Dutch *Sint Maarten* is the smallest inhabited island in the world that is shared by two nations. Located in the Caribbean, approximately 300 km east of Puerto Rico, it has a population of roughly 80,000 inhabitants. The eighty-seven-square-kilometre island is divided roughly sixty-forty between France and the Netherlands, with roughly equal population on both sides. The capital cities are Philipsburg (Dutch) and Marigot (French). The island is hilly and has no rivers, so just like Bermuda it relies on the rains for water. The neighbouring island include Anguilla, St Barts, and Saba, with many of the more distant islands visible on clear days. It has a tropical monsoon climate, with a dry season from January to April and a rainy season from August to December, with temperatures stable throughout the year that rarely exceed 34°C or fall below 20°C. St Maarten's Dutch side is known for its festive nightlife, beaches, jewellery, drinks made with native rum-based guava berry liquors, and casinos. The island's French side is known for its nude beaches, clothes, shopping, and French and Indian Caribbean cuisine. St. Maarten attracts tourists from across the world. The short runway at the international airport, positioned between a large hill and a beach, create some spectacular approaches. Aviation photographers flock to the airport to capture pictures of large jets just a few meters above sunbathers on Maho Beach.

As we came in for the landing, this view of Maho Beach and its sunbathers, was our first sighting of St Maarten. Upon our arrival at the terminal building, we were met by the hotel limo driver and taken to Port de Plaisance, as the resort was called, for it had not yet acquired the Sheraton name. We would occupy a suite there for about a month until we eventually found the house we rented about two kilometres from the resort.

It was early October 1991, and Shelley and I were happy to be back on a tropical Caribbean island and avoiding the upcoming Canadian winter. Although we loved Canada, and the province of Nova Scotia in particular, Canadian winters are both long and severe. The company agreed to ship all our furniture and our sailboat, which eventually arrived, and we moored the boat in the resort marina, moved the furniture into the newly rented home, and settled in for the duration, however long or short that may be. Unusually, this contract was open-ended and not the two years that was commonly used for expatriate postings.

Set in lush, tropical gardens with views of the blue-green waters and majestic hills, the luxurious Port de Plaisance already offered eighty-eight elegantly appointed timeshare suites spread over several three-storey villas, surrounding a seventy-slip yacht club, and five restaurants, all located on the edge of the large lagoon. The plans called for considerable further development, and Sheraton won the bid to manage the project as it moved towards completion. Eventually, it would consist of a five-hundred-room hotel, several restaurants, a unique conference centre with moving floors allowing for the conversion from theatre seating to banquet seating in minutes, a twelve-thousand-square-foot Monte Carlo-style casino, complemented by a gourmet night club with A-list international acts, a state-of-the-art spa and health club, seven tennis courts lighted for night play, and several swimming pools. This was to be enhanced by floodlit fountains in the centre of the lagoon. It was to be a billion-dollar project and Sheraton's flagship resort. With so much to offer, Sheraton Port de Plaisance would be the most luxurious full-featured resort located on the island of St. Maarten, or indeed, anywhere in the Caribbean.

Early on the morning of their first day, I walked to the site office building to meet with Ed. Pinczowski, who was Sheraton's general manager for the property. Ed was the only Sheraton employee on site at that time and was happy to have me join him as the second Sheraton member of staff. While there were several components of the resort already operational, those were managed by the developer Alain Christian, and the employees reported to him.

Sheraton's management agreement with the owning company, which was a French pension and insurance conglomerate, was not yet in place. Shelley and I were to spend the next two and a half years on the island of St. Maarten, and we were to experience a cornucopia of the bizarre, beginning the very next day.

"Welcome to St Maarten, Colm. I'm very glad you're here and look forward to us working together"; was Ed's warm and friendly greeting. I instantly liked my new boss, and over time, we became friends.

Great tragedy befell Ed and his wife, Marjan, more than twenty years later when their only two children, whom we had known as tiny tots, now in their twenties, were killed by a terrorist bomb in Brussels Airport.

"Colm, let's tour the property, and we can talk as we walk":

Ed clarified the relation between himself representing Sheraton and Alain Christian, the developer, who represented the owning company and was responsible for seeing the project to completion, in readiness for Sheraton to manage.

"As general manager, I'm really in the planning stage of how we should operate as a Sheraton resort of quality. Alain Christian's staff run the components of the resort that are currently functioning, and I have limited input except where situations arise that might impact the interests of Sheraton when we are fully responsible for the property. And we sometimes 'butt heads' over issues" Ed explained.

"Anyway, Colm, tomorrow we'll attend an operations meeting, chaired by Alain. That will give you some idea of the current 'state of play', and you'll get to meet the heads of the various departments. Let's go back to the site office, and I'll show you your office, and you can start to settle in."

With that, my responsibilities as director of human resources for the Sheraton Port de Plaisance Resort and Casino Sint Maarten began.

The following morning, at the appointed time of nine a.m., Ed and I made our way to the large conference room in the site office for the operations meeting. There were several dozen department managers and assistants in attendance. We were really there as observers as Sheraton currently had little or no operational input. I had never experienced a meeting conducted in this style before. Alain Christian, seated at the head of the U-shaped table setup, asked each manager in turn to stand and present a report on the performance of their department since the last meeting. Reasonable enough! He followed this by asking the department manager to publicly evaluate his or her assistants' performance, including any weaknesses or failings, concurrently identifying any problem employees in their department. Maybe not quite so reasonable! As if this was not already bizarre enough, he subsequently turned to the assistant and ask him or her to stand and, in front of their colleagues, evaluate their boss's performance in managing their department. This was definitely not at all reasonable! This went on all day, and the sense of embarrassment and humiliation that pervaded the room was toxic. By six pm, I had had enough. I turned towards Ed and told him I no longer wished to continue in this meeting. With Ed in agreement, both of us quietly slipped out of the room. The following morning, I learned the meeting had concluded at about ten p.m., and this was indicative of the management style that continued until Sheraton was fully responsible for the property.

My early tasks were to set up the human resources systems, prepare the corporate HR policies and procedures for when Sheraton would take over the resort, hire some administrative help, begin to develop staffing guides by department, and identify markets to obtain the professional expatriate staff I needed to find from abroad. This would take at least the first six months of my time, and I started by identifying an administrative assistant who could help in setting up the HR systems. The resort developers had hired a USA-based security company headed up by two retired FBI agents, and they assisted me in developing a drug policy and background check procedure for all new employees. All gaming staff had to be licensed by the gaming authority, and all staff had to have an international background check. Many decades earlier, organised crime had lost control of the casino industry to corporate America. Since then, the industry internationally, with a few exceptions, has been very highly regulated. With such vast amounts of cash in circulation in a labour-intensive business, the potential for illicit activity is neutralized through the use of extremely detailed and highly technical security systems and procedures.

I had used a couple of North American-based employment agencies in the past, and I asked them to 'head hunt' several senior positions for me, which they successfully did, with staff coming from Canada, USA, Korea, and Europe soon joining the resort. The senior casino staff would all come from Sheraton's only casino at that time, which was in Townsville, Australia.

Not all the arrivals of expatriate staff to St Maarten went smoothly, however. For political reason, foreign employees where advised that their work permits would be issued when they were already on the island and that at airport immigration, they should just say they were on a visit.

The food and beverage director, an American from Miami, in his wisdom, however, decided he would say he was there to work at the new Sheraton Port de Plaisance. Without a work permit, he, his wife, and his small daughter were immediately turned around and sent back to Puerto Rico, the nearest US territory. Upon hearing this, an urgent and exceptional appeal was made to the authorities, and his work permit was immediately issued. Shelley agreed to fly with it to Puerto Rico and bring the lost sheep back to the fold.

December of 1991, Erika decided to visit from London, where she'd lived since leaving Bermuda some years earlier. Shelley and I were of course delighted to see her, and while she never said so directly, it appeared to us that she was having some difficulties with a relationship she was in. We were concerned for her and hoped she would stay on in St Maarten, as she had no particular reason to return to London. Erika joined the dealer classes being run for the casino and stayed for a couple of months, but she eventually went back to the UK.

As there were already several casinos in St Maarten, operations staff, such as dealers, slot machine technicians, cashiers, and other gaming employees, would be locally hired and trained to Sheraton standards. As soon as Sheraton triggered their management contract and their management team was in place, all existing staff that worked for the developer would be terminated. They would then be given the opportunity to interview for the same or different positions as Sheraton employees. In order to ensure as smooth a transition as possible, no announcement would be made until the day the interviewing, firing, and hiring occurred.

I carefully choreographed the process and early in 1992, on the day appointed, the Sheraton managers were advised in a meeting what was to happen and their role in it, which was to interview and rehire those staff members they wished to have in their departments. The plan was immediately implemented, and while there were approximately three hundred employees affected, all went as well as could be expected. There were some shocks, though, and in some cases, anger reared its ugly head. While the majority were rehired, some were not, and some were offered different positions than they had held previously. The public relations staff managed the media and public perceptions, and Port de Plaisance became Sheraton Port de Plaisance.

Construction of the core component of the resort, the hotel and conference centre, had not as yet begun. However, to impress and reassure owning company executives who visited the island on occasion, Alain Christian would put on a great show of ongoing construction where none actually existed. He hired several trucks and had them load up with dirt at one spot and move it to a second location, unload, reload, and move the dirt back again. All this trucking activity seemed to reassure the owners that progress was being made.

One morning, as I arrived to work, I looked into Ed's office to say good morning. Ed didn't look happy; in fact, he looked quite upset.

"Did you see the local papers, Colm?" he asked.

"Here, have a look!"

"Oh my God". I responded in shock.

There, on the front page, the bold headline screamed out: "Excessive Payment to Expats at Sheraton Port de Plaisance". This was followed by intimate and comprehensive details of tax-free salaries, housing allowances, foreign services allowances, car allowances, and food allowances for all the resort's expatriate management staff. For their willingness to live on an island away from home, the expatriates were very well compensated, and the gap between them and local staff was considerable. This information could only have come from the human resources department. While the resort's public relations staff went into spin mode, the damage was done. I immediately dismissed my administrative assistant after she admitted she'd leaked the information. It was a damning display of irresponsibility and disloyalty! While the information embarrassed me, as it was inevitably at my desk where this particular buck stopped. It also generated considerable gossip around the island over the next couple of weeks, but with an effective level of active spin from the public relations staff, it eventually died down and was forgotten.

We had a wonderful social life in St Maarten. Sundays were frequently spent on Pinel Island, a ten-minute boat ride just off the French side, or on Orient Beach, also on the French side. Lunches or dinners in Margot, or in one of the many restaurants on the Dutch side of the island were regular occurances.

In marketing St Maarten as a luxury destination, several big-name acts were contracted to perform in various resorts, including Port de Plaisance. Bill Cosby, the now disgraced comedian, although not so at the time, and Chaka Khan were two acts that headlined at Port de Plaisance, and Shelley and I had the opportunity to attend concerts in other resorts featuring the legendary jazz musicians Dave Brubeck and Lionel Hampton. Shelley volunteered her free time with the small zoo on the island, and she and I made several friends locally.

One of our first social events was for the recently arrived Australian casino management team. As director of human resources, I felt responsible for ensuring that all expatriate staff were welcomed to the resort and to the island, and Shelley and I decided to throw a party at our home for the Australians. A plentiful supply of food and drinks were available, and on the appointed evening, the Australian managers and their wives arrived, about a dozen people in total. They all carried small coolers, and when seated on our patio, the coolers were placed beside them.

"What can I get everyone to drink"?

I enquired of our guests. They silently reacted by dipping into their coolers for their own supply. At the end of what was a pleasant enough evening, they took their coolers and what was left of their adult beverages with them and departed. *Strange*, I thought. This appeared to be a cultural norm in Australia.

Sailing *Sherco*, our sailboat, which we had frequently enjoyed in Nova Scotia, was somewhat challenging, and it got little use during our time in St Maarten. The resort's marina, where it was moored, was inside the large lagoon with only one channel to the open sea, over which there was a small drawbridge on the busy main road leading to the airport. Because of frequent flights in and out of St Maarten and the heavy traffic that this produced, the bridge was only opened twice a day, at six thirty am and at six thirty pm, for about fifteen minutes each time. Timing was all-important. So, the majority of any sailing we did was usually just inside the lagoon.

As our second Christmas in Sint Maarten approached, the Christmas of 1992, I began to feel unwell, and one day, I collapsed in my office. Ed, whose office was adjacent, heard the thud and immediately went to investigate. The door was locked, and maintenance was called. Opening it, they found me unconscious on the floor. I was exhausted, and taking Christmas off work, I flew alone to the neighbouring island of Saba to rest and relax for a few days over the holiday period.

Saba consists largely of the volcanic "Mount Scenery". At 887 metres, the now extinct volcano is the highest point within all the territories of The Netherlands, including, of course, the flat topography of Holland itself. The vegetation of Saba is mainly composed of woodland forest, with ferns, damp soil, and many mango trees. Visitors refer to Saba's forest as "the Elfin Forest" because of its high altitude, mist, and mossy appearance and the island's lush plant and animal wildlife that is so diverse. Because of its tiny size, the population of Saba is only about two thousand, consisting of a small number of island families.

The flight to Saba from St Maarten is only twelve minutes in a tiny sixteen-seat turbo-prop aircraft, dwarfed by the larger international jet aircraft at the airport. The landing on Saba's airport runway, which is only four hundred meters long and reputed to be one of the trickiest and most dangerous in the world, was a white-knuckle experience, with the plane stopping just meters from the end of the runway, just before a drop-off straight into the sea.

I walked from the small terminal building to the tiny resort, appropriately sized for the island. I would spend three days reading, hiking the mountain up into the tropical misty rain forest at the summit, resting, eating, and drinking well, in preparation for my return to St Maarten and to the upcoming tasks ahead.

Back on St Maarten for the beginning of 1993, wondering what unusual events the coming year promised, I, well rested and recovered from my earlier scare, settled back into my routine, although 'routine' might be a misnomer when applied to Port de Plaisance. Since early 1992, when Sheraton implemented their management contract, the casino had been open, and it was now fully operational, as was the supporting supper club. I had identified an excellent spa director from California who was now running the luxury spa operation, beauty salon, swimming pools, and tennis centre. Alain Christians continued to be on site as the construction of the hotel and conference centre were still to begin.

About mid-year, I experienced some health problems. I generally felt unwell and suffered from dizzy spells. In light of my recent incident, collapsing in my office and the transient ischemic attack (TIA) of a few years earlier in Nova Scotia, I took no chances. Health facilities in St Maarten were very limited, and after a thorough examination, my doctor decided I should go to Puerto Rico for further tests. I immediately took a flight, checked into the hospital, had the tests, including a rather painful spinal tap, and returned to St Maarten to await the results. In due course, they arrived, and no problem had been identified, but the appropriate precaution had been taken.

The Port de Plaisance circus continued unabated, with no sign of construction of the hotel starting. According to a very reliable grapevine, some 350 million dollars had already been invested in the infrastructure and the currently functioning departments. While we continued to enjoy our time there, taking trips to St Barts and Anguilla, and Shelley travelling, along with a girlfriend, to Curacao, Sheraton corporate started to question the slow pace of development. It had been two years since their management contract had been put in place, with still no progress on the hotel, the central core of the resort.

December of that year, Erika returned to St Maarten for a visit to introduce her fiancée, Simon Fallon. He seemed a pleasant, outgoing, and personable individual, and the initial impression was reasonably positive. He was sixteen years older than Erika, which was a concern in itself, but that paled in comparison to the news we heard next, that he had been married twice before. We attempted to discourage the relationship, but 'love is blind' and with Simon's assurance that Erika would be loved and taken care of, we had no option but to accept the situation, hoping he would be true to his word. Erika and Simon returned to London with parental acceptance, if not exactly parental agreement. They are now divorced.

Random drug testing of staff was a feature of their employment and a clause in their employment contract, which stated they would comply when requested. This was done through hair testing, as hair maintained trace evidence of drug use for up to three months and was more effective than urine testing. The use of drugs was grounds for immediate dismissal, and the vast majority of the employees took no chances, although there had been the odd employee who failed a test and was dismissed. On one particular occasion early in 1994, when a random drug test was administered, a casino dealer who had a reputation as an aggressive, undisciplined employee was identified with cocaine in his system. Upon receiving the report, I informed the casino manager, Rod Woolley, who was this employee's boss, and as the policy dictated, he would have to be sacked. He was called into my office just before the start of his daytime shift, and Rod and I informed him that he had failed a drug test and was now immediately dismissed from the company in compliance with policy. Not unexpectedly, his reaction was threatening and aggressive, and he had to be escorted off the property by security. Later that morning, as I was engrossed in work at my desk with the office door open, I heard the door quietly click shut, and looking up, saw the angry, distorted, disdainful look on the face of the dealer who had been terminated from his position just a few hours earlier.

"What are you doing here"? I enquired.

"I need my job"

"You should have thought of that before using drugs. How did you get in anyway!"

In a quietly menacing voice, as a feeling of dread overcame me, and he slowly pulled a large kitchen knife out from under his jacket and held it at arm's length, pointing it at my head while moving towards me, he demanded;

"Get me my job back."

In a sudden movement, the knife was right at my head, and while I managed to deflect it, I was forced to assure the individual,

"Okay, okay, you'll get your job back. Report for the next shift. I'll sort it out".

Surprisingly, immediately satisfied with my assurance, he quickly left as I collapsed in shock on the floor and called out to my staff. A large cognac was sent for, and with nerves settled, I instructed one of the staff to have the security consultants inform the police. That individual never returned to the resort.

Shelley and I, along with Rod Woolley and his wife, Suzanne, were immediately secreted off to a remote resort on the French side of the island as a precaution. The police began an island-wide search for the perpetrator of what was now considered attempted murder. The four of us remained in seclusion for a couple of days, grateful for the opportunity to relax, or try to at least, away from the daily work stresses and the incident I had experienced. I knew that our security company would keep the pressure on the police to apprehend the culprit.

Subsequently, we returned to the Dutch side, and as the attacker was not yet apprehended, Rod and I were assigned bodyguards. Pierre was an ex-French Foreign Legionnaire assigned to guard me. He would sit outside our house at night, armed of course, drive me to work in the morning, collect me from work in the evening, and again remain at the house overnight. This routine continued for about a week until, one morning, the police came to my office to inform me they had apprehended the culprit and needed me to go to the police station to identify both him and the weapon. That itself was an unnerving experience as I began to shake uncontrolably when I saw the knife, but with that done, it was time to move on. Pierre's services were no longer required, and we parted company. He had kept us safe, and although we'd only known each other for that week, there was an emotional dimension to the farewell, undoubtedly precipitated by the trauma of the incident.

Nan Palmer, Divisional Vice President of Human Resources, decide that after this event, Shelley and I should go and stay at the Sheraton Miami Beach Hotel in Florida for rest and relaxation. I readily agreed, as everything about Port de Plaisance, the knife attack, the continuous non-start of the final components of the resort, and island phobia had begun to crowd in on me. Both my time and my interest in St. Maarten had their ends in sight.

Upon returning from Miami after a week, two possible opportunities for transfer were presented to me. The first one the company asked me to consider was as director of human resources for the Sheraton Hotel in Long Beach, California. I flew out to meet with the general manager of the hotel, spent a couple of days familiarising myself with the hotel and with the area, and soon decided this place was not for me. Returning to St. Maarten, the next potential position available was a dream location. It was the Sheraton Resort on the island of Maui in the Hawaiian Islands, one of Sheraton's most luxurious resorts in the world, on one of the world's most beautiful islands. While the position was mine for the taking, the hotel would not pay to ship my sailboat all the way from the Caribbean to Hawaii. There was no market for my boat in St Maarten, and I was left with no option but to forgo Maui and await another opportunity, a huge disappointment. I had invested twenty five thousand dollars in my sailboat and could not afford to just abandon her. And she was too small to take on the Pacific Ocean, a long way from St. Maarten to Hawaii.

It was now the spring of 1994, and sometime earlier, Sheraton had purchased Caesars World Inc., the company that owned and operated the world-famous Caesars Palace in Las Vegas and its newer sister, Caesars in Atlantic City. This move was Sheraton's foray into the lucrative casino industry on mainland USA. With Mississippi recently passing legislation to permit casinos in Tunica County, a Sheraton casino was currently ready to start operating there. I was asked if it would interest me to relocate to Tunica, I agreed to do so..

As we prepared to leave St. Maarten, we sold the car and furniture and packed up our personal effects, and I arranged to have a friend, Mike Nolan, along with a local young man as crew, sail our boat from St Maarten to Florida. This was a voyage that 'Sherco' could handle, a very much shorter distance than to Maui. So, after almost three years, in early April of 1994, we left an incomplete Sheraton Port de Plaisance and St Maarten on a flight to Memphis, Tennessee.

A few years later, Sheraton terminated their management agreement with Port de Plaisance as the property was never completed. It was subsequently sold for an estimated $40 million after $350 million had been invested in it. I later heard that Alain Christian, the developer, was tried and convicted of fraud in France. About a decade later, after I retired from Sheraton, a decision I sometimes regretted, I was offered a job back in St. Maarten as director of training at the Maho Beach resort. I returned to St Maarten but remained for only a month as both the island and the work had now lost their appeal.

Shelley and friend Inge at Sheraton St Maarten

Shelley and I on Pinel Island, St Maarten

Chapter Fourteen
Mississippi, Tunica Casino

Shortly before finally departing St Maarten, I flew to Las Vegas to meet with Caesars World's vice president of human resources. I was booked into the famous Desert Inn. The hotel was full, and no regular rooms were available, so they checked me into the presidential suite, ten thousand square feet of decadent luxury. As I stood on the balcony of this two storey suite with its wall to ceiling windows overlooking the golf course and it's grand piano now standing silently below in the livingroom, I reminised on it's past occupants, many, the idols of my youth.

My love for the industry I spent my life working in, living in, and yes loving in, my pride in the company I now worked for, encourages me to relate a brief story of this American original and truly iconic resort, now a part of 'our company'. In it's heyday you could see Frank Sinatra and the Rat Pack or Elvis while enjoying dinner or drinks here.

The Desert Inn on the 'Las Vegas Strip', opened on April 24, 1950. Renowned for its opulence during the 1950s, the hotel frequently hosted, such guests as Senetor J.F.Kennedy, Winston Churchill, and President Harry S. Truman. Frank Sinatra made his Las Vegas debut in 1951 and became a regular performer at the Desert Inn.

Almost every major star of the latter half of the 20th century played at the Desert Inn in its famous Crystal Showroom. They included Patti Page, Bobby Darin, Jimmy Durante, Tony Bennett, Paul Anka, Dionne Warwick, Louise Mandrell, Noël Coward, Benny Goodman, Dinah Shore Rosemary Clooney and many many more. Wayne Newton was the resident 'king of entertainment' at the resort, earning $10 million a year, which made him the highest paid nightclub performer of all time. In 1992, Frank Sinatra celebrated his 77th birthday in a glittering star studded event at the hotel, which had been his entertainment   'home away from home' for many years.

The Desert Inn's most famous owner Howard Hughes, purchased the resort from Mafia gang lord Dalitz during the Mafia's period in control of Las Vegas prior to the 1970s, when corporate America moved in and legitimised casino gambling.

After Hughes's death in 1976, the hotel was sold to Kirk Kerkorian and Kerkorian sold it to Sheraton Hotels in 1993 for $160 million. Four years later in 1997, Sheraton Hotels spent $200 million on renovating the Desert Inn.

On April 27, 2000 Steve Wynn a Las Vegas casino mogul and the owner of several resorts in the city, purchased the resort from Sheraton for $270 million and he closed it one day later at 2:00 a.m. on August 28, 2000. Subsequently, the world famous Desert Inn Resort and Casino, Las Vegas was imploded to make room for a mega resort that Wynn would build.

The closure and demolition of the Desert Inn in 2000 marked the end of old Las Vegas, as the heavily tourism-driven modern Las Vegas subsequently emerged.

Sheraton Casino Tunica, Mississippi, was to be directly managed by Caesars World, so I was transferred from Sheraton payroll to Caesars payroll, hence the need for this meeting in Las Vegas. I had taken a backward career step, accepting the role of director of training and development. As this was a domestic position, not an expatriate one, there was no contractual period, with the job considered 'open-ended' and all expatriate allowances disappearing. It would, however, keep me in the casino division, with earnings considerably more lucrative than in the hotel division, and the work itself, in many ways, was more fun.

The casino in Tunica was a considerably larger operation than Port de Plaisance, administered by an experienced team of American casino managers. It would be staffed by some two thousand line employees, all local Mississippians, inexperienced both in the casino industry specifically and, in many cases, the world of work generally. Many had never previously been employed and would require extensive, intense, and in-depth training, both in the norms of customer service and the skills of their individual jobs.

I was the only one from St Maarten offered a position in the Tunica casino. In fact, I was one of only a very few Sheraton employees from anywhere in the company transferred to Tunica. Of course, it was largely because this was Sheraton's first casino anywhere in the world, apart from the small one they had in Townsville, Australia, and the one in St Maarten, which had a rather doubtful future. Gaming staff within the company, therefore, were few, as the Australians from St Maarten eventually returned to Australia. There were, of course, very experienced casino staff in Sheraton's new acquisition, Caesars Palace, but the likelihood of anyone wishing to leave Las Vegas for Tunica was extremely remote.

In my new position, I would spearhead the implementation of Sheraton's unique service culture, SGSS, the Sheraton Guest Satisfaction System. In this cornucopia of the experiential and cultural, with much of the line more comfortable picking cotton, fishing for catfish, or shooting game and some of the management staff more dictatorial than consultative, this was a challenge! Tunica County, Mississippi, epitomised the commonly held image of the 'Deep South' of America.

The law confines casinos to waters along the Mississippi River and in navigable waters of counties bordering the river. Mississippi law also requires that casino riverboats be permanently moored at the dock, and they are not permitted to cruise. This allows the riverboats to offer twenty-four-hour dockside gambling. Since the law does not require that the floating vessel actually resemble a boat, almost all of the casinos are built on barges. This gives them the appearance of a land-based building rather than a riverboat.

Tunica's first casino, Splash, opened a few years earlier at Mhoon Landing in October 1992. It was a small casino atop a barge, in effect a floating nightclub, and people would queue for hours to gain admission. It was rumoured, which may have been an "urban myth", that it made so much money that they would take it to the bank in barrels. Their construction method became the model for all casinos in Tunica County. The casino companies excavated huge channels from the Mississippi River or it's navigable tributaries, connecting excavated lakes they had also created, and floated massive freight barges capable of carrying thousands of tons through the channels and into these artificial lakes. Then they closed them off and refilled the channels. They then anchored the barges and filled in the lake to the edge of the barge, and while the barge floated, it was for all intents and purposes land-based. They built the casinos on top of these barges, with surrounding car parks, roadways, gardens, and walkways!

Prior to Splash Casino, Tunica County had an unemployment rate of twenty-six percent and was the poorest county in the whole of the United States. At the time Sheraton decided to acquire Caesars World and build a casino in Tunica County, development of the industry was explosive, with most of the major casino resort companies from Las Vegas jumping on the bandwagon, and tens of thousands of new jobs were created. Sheraton Casino, Circus Circus Casino, and Horseshoe Casino were close to each other and combined resources to create a casino park, which they named Tunica Casino Centre, a basic, simple name, but one which proved to be very effective marketing. They built a three-mile access road off Highway 61, which snaked its way from Memphis, Tennessee, their primary market down through Mississippi, off to their three casinos at Casino Centre.

The centre was nearer to Memphis than Splash, and when Sheraton Casino opened, it captured a substantial portion of that market. Eventually, other major casino companies from Las Vegas moved into Mhoon Landing, further down Highway 61. The forerunner of it all, Splash, was unable to compete with the wealth and power of Las Vegas, and it closed its doors.

Shelley's and my arrival in Memphis Airport, back on 'domestic soil', was somewhat reminiscent of our arrival in Hamburg some two decades earlier: no one to meet us now as it was then. Reservations had been made for us at a Holiday Inn in downtown Memphis! Thus was the tribulation of a 'domestic posting'.

I had earlier received instructions on how to report for work, and on the day following our arrival, I rented a car and travelled down the notorious, though famous, Highway 61 to Casino Centre, a distance of about sixty miles from Memphis. U.S Highway 61, known as the 'blues highway', rivals Route 66 as the most famous road in American music folklore. A vast number of blues artists have recorded songs about Highway 61, including many Mississippians. Travel was a popular theme in blues music, and highways have symbolized the potential to quickly 'pack up and go', leave troubles behind, or seek out new opportunities elsewhere. As the major route northward out of Mississippi, US Highway 61 has been an inspiration to blues artists wishing to expand their musical influence. The road begins in downtown New Orleans and travels through Baton Rouge, into Mississippi, up to Tunica, on to Memphis, and continues north to the Canadian border. Mississippi artists who lived near Highway 61 include BB King, Muddy Waters, Ike Turner, Sam Cooke, and many more. In 1965, the road gained a further mythological reputation when Bob

Dylan recorded his influential album *Highway 61 Revisited*. But the section of the highway I was to become familiar with, between Memphis and the casinos in Tunica, was a meandering two-lane death trap, compounded by the exponential growth in traffic from Memphis to the casinos, particularly at night. In recent years, however, Highway 61 has been expanded and improved.

The human resources director who introduced me to the general manager, other members of the management team, and Glen Campbell—no, not that Glen Campbell—greeted my arrival at the casino warmly. Glen Campbell was on temporary assignment from Sheraton Headquarters Human Resources Department to assist during the casino opening. He had been in Tunica for about six months and had become familiar with Memphis, Tunica, and the county. He would help me settle into my new role, show me around, and suggest some of the more desirable residential parts of Memphis where Shelley and I might like to live.

On one of our first forays out of the casino on a mini-Tunica-familiarisation tour, Glen suggested,

"Okay Colm, come on, we're going for a drive, so you can experience some Tunica culture."

We drove back out onto Highway 61, moving south for about twenty miles, and turned onto a narrow dirt road toward the levy, that huge bank of earth that ran along the side of the Mississippi River wherever it might flood. It was starting to get hot, and the humidity was rising. Mississippi is hot in summer and cool in the winter.

"Let's go," said Glen as we got out of the car and climbed up sod steps hewn out of the side of the levy. From atop, we could see on the Mississippi River side of the levy what appeared to be a village of homes—shacks in reality—built on stilts to protect them from the rising of the river waters. The social centre of this 'village' was a cheaply constructed wooden structure, a bar, a fact indicated by the red neon sign advertising Budweiser, which hung askew over the entrance. Access was gained from the top of the levy to this 'building' by a planked, somewhat rickety walkway, also on stilts.

We gingerly made our way forward, entered the bar, and sat at the counter. "Two Buds, please." The inside was small, cluttered with basic wooden chairs and tables and a well-used pool table at one end, yet it was not entirely uncomfortable. However, the same could not be said of the atmosphere. The two strangers in business clothes were not greeted with open arms, and welcome smiles. The few bearded, large, and intimidating-looking locals viewed us with suspicion, curiosity, or both. They just looked—rather, stared— but didn't speak. We were somewhat intimidated, made no attempt to initiate conversation, and the 'Buds' were quickly consumed, and departure undertaken. Local Tunica culture had been experienced.

Even though Memphis was a relatively long distance to drive back and forth to work each day, the town of Tunica would not have been considered one of the more desirable places to live. It wasn't really a town, more akin to an industrial area with several ramshackle industrial building, a number of small homes, one or two much larger, gaudy ones, undoubtedly owned by the local bigwigs, kingpins, or politicians, a greasy spoon restaurant called Rosie's, some seedy bars hidden away, and the railway track that ran alongside the main street. In Tunica, one could conjure up visions of the movies '*In the Heat of the Night*', or '*Cat on a Hot Tin Roof*'.

I returned the rental car and purchased a new Toyota Corolla, reliable for the daily round trip of 120 miles to and from work. Then Shelley and I set about the task of searching for a home. At that time, there was no expectation of any further move. Would we never learn? We decided we would purchase a home rather than rent. Our financial health had been greatly restored since the earlier loss of our business interest in Canada, due to our exceptional earning ability while in both Bermuda and St Maarten. We could afford to be choosy and would pay cash for the right property. We eventually found a beautiful, three-thousand-square-foot American Colonial-style house on about half an acre, with a swimming pool, in the very nice neighbourhood of Fox Meadows, West Memphis.

Our personal effects arrived from St Maarten, and we once again began furniture shopping, a familiar activity since we had done this on so many previous occasions, tending to sell rather than ship furniture when moving. Pete and Marge Harris, an elderly couple who lived opposite our new home, befriended us and were extremely helpful. Pete even helped me with gardening and lent me his tools.

'Sherco' our sailboat arrived in Florida, having been sailed from St. Maarten, and she was hauled out of the water, lifted onto a boat truck trailer, and moved to Tennessee. Then she was offloaded into Lake Barclay, about three hours' drive from Memphis. While an inconvenient location, it was the nearest suitably sized body of water. However, because of distance and my very full schedule pre-opening of the casino, there was no opportunity to sail her.

With two thousand employees to train in Sheraton's corporate service philosophy, I developed and implemented a three-day orientation program. Management and supervision received a one-day summarised version.

The opening day of Sheraton Casino Tunica, Mississippi, arrived, and so did the customers, cars, and coach tours, largely from Memphis, but also from all over Mississippi and Tennessee. The casino was open twenty-four hours a day, and on opening day, thirty thousand people passed through its doors. It was 'all hands on deck' for that day, and administrative, functional, and support staff, as well as the operational employees, were corralled into duty on the floor. I spent the day out in the Mississippi sun, supervising the concierge staff that were directing traffic, which was backed up the three-mile Casino Centre Road to Highway 61.

The Sheraton Casino Tunica would continue to be successful over the years that followed, however, it would go through several different ownerships.

Life assumed a regular routine, as with most people: weekdays for work and weekends for play. While Nashville in the north of Tennessee was considered the home of country music, Memphis, in the south, bordering the states of Mississippi, and Arkansas across the river, was the home of the delta blues, and Beale Street was its heart.

While I was extremely busy in the early stages of the casino pre and post-opening and didn't always have a full weekend off, Shelley and I did manage to have some cultural and social life. The highlight of early summer was the Memphis in May Festival. It was held throughout the month, beginning on the first weekend with the three-day Beale Street Music Festival, and in 1994, it was headlined by such artists as Bob Dylan, the Isley Brothers, Buddy Guy, Joan Baez, Percy Sledge, Jimmy Rodgers, and many more. Work, unfortunately, precluded our attendance at the BSMF, as it was commonly called. However, subsequent visits to Beale Street to enjoy blues music with ribs and beer at BB King's Blues Club or Mr Handy's Blues Bar and others along the street were certainly memorable experiences.

One Sunday during the Memphis in May festival, we spent the day in Tom Lee Park, where the World Championship Barbecue Cooking Contest takes place. It was a beautiful clear sunny day and the smell of BBQ meats, as we slowly wandered along the pathway at the edge of the might Mississippi river, all combined to hone our appetites. This is a phenomenal event where some three hundred huge BBQs compete in several categories, including whole hogs, pork shoulders, ribs, and a variety of other cuts of meat. Tom Lee Park is a thirty-three-acre park on the banks of the Mississippi River, located on Riverside Drive, between Beale Street and

Georgia Avenue.

Memphis is a truly iconic American city, where musical artists of all genres come to pay homage to its blues heritage, and in 1994, we took the opportunity to attend at least some of their concerts: Bette Midler at the Pyramid Arena in June, The Moody Blues on Mud Island on the Arkansas side of the Mississippi River in July, and Johnny Mathis and Julio Iglesias on other occasions. We also listened to great artists in jazz clubs along Beale Street. Not only was Memphis the home of the delta blues, but it was also the birthplace of rock 'n roll, with Sam Phillip's Sun Studio its mother. Shelley and I felt privilaged to set our feet upon this special place. We were surprised to see how small the studio was, number 706 on the corner of Union Avenue, yet how important, how iconic, it was the place from whence all modern rock music originally emanated. Elvis Presley began his career there, as did Johnny Cash, Jerry Lee Lewis, Roy Orbison, Carl Perkins, BB King, and many more. It is now designated as a 'National Heritage Landmark'.

Our visit to Graceland, Elvis Presley's home, was a quiet reflective encounter with the memories of our youth. The music of Elvis, and other artists that came out of Memphis had been a huge influence during our teenage years.

Arguably the music of the time had a greater impact on our generation, than on any other since. This new 'rebellious' music, or rather, old blues music in brand new clothes, helped fuel a seismic shift in attitude from our parents pre-WW2 generation, and the 'war baby' and baby boomer generation, those of us born during the war and directly after it, and our rebellion against previously held social norms. We were the first generation, not yet adults, but no longer children, a new generation called 'teenagers'.

My fifty second birthday, June 16, 1994, was a Thursday. As it was a work day and I usually arrived home late in the evening, Shelley and I decided that we would wait until Friday night to celebrate and go out for dinner. On the evening of June 17, 1994, as planned, we left for O'Charley's, which was a popular chain of steak and seafood restaurants across America, and our local one was about a ten-minute walk from home. As usual for a Friday night, the place was packed, but the usual chatter of voices and clatter of cutlery and crockery was strangely missing, while the crowd was transfixed as they viewed the TV behind the bar.

"What's going on?" I asked a nearby customer.

" OJ Simpson's on the run. Apparently he murdered his ex-wife. That's what they're reporting anyway"

OJ Simpson was arguably one of the most renowned football players, then retired, in America sporting history. This TV transmission was live, as it was happening, the white Bronco SUV moving down the highway in California, and now Shelley and I were also sucked into this transfixion. Dinner was eaten very late that evening.

Shortly afterwards, OJ Simpson was charged with the murders of his ex-wife, Nicole Brown Simpson, and Ronald Goldman, the event turned into a manhunt as Simpson went missing and was declared a fugitive. Hours later, the infamous low-speed chase began. Approximately six forty-five pm, California time, on June 17, 1994, police saw Simpson on the expressway in a white Ford Bronco driven by his best friend, Al Cowlings. Simpson was riding in the back and reportedly had a gun. With the cavalcade of police cars in pursuit, TV helicopters swooped in to join the chase. The sixty-mile, low-speed pursuit through southern Los Angeles, along with his eventual trial, would go down as two of the most watched events in television history.

Summer turned to autumn, autumn turned to winter, the air chilled, and the grass frosted. The swimming pool was covered, and I drove to Barclay Lake to prepare *Sherco*, our sailboat, to weather the coming winter. We had not sailed her once that past summer and I was looking forward to next year and making a more concerted effort to sail Barclay Lake aboard our boat, along with participating in the other activities of the glorious spring and summer of 1995 in Memphis, Tennessee.

But Caesars World had other ideas!

"Colm, I'll be in Tunica early next week, and we'll meet, okay." It was early January 1995, and the brief phone call was from Kathy Moore, Caesars corporate vice president of human resources. We met, and Kathy had a proposal—well, they were always presented as proposals or suggestions, but in many cases, were actually instructions.

"Colm, Nova Scotia government has passed legislation permiting two casinos, one in Halifax and a smaller one in Sydney, Cape Breton, and we've won the contract to operate them. we would like to transfer you back to Nova Scotia."

The plan was that I would open the Sydney Casino as Personnel Director, and simultaneously, the Halifax Casino would be opened with Sherri LeClair, a long-term, very experienced, and competent American Sheraton employee, as Human Resources Director. Within approximately a year after opening, when systems, policies, and procedures were in place in both casinos, Sherri would relocate back to the USA, and I would move to Halifax as Vice President of Human Resources for the two casinos and the Sheraton Hotel.

On this occasion, I was happy to be the recipient of the proposal, the severity of winter ignored. We loved Canada, and Nova Scotia in particular. Because we had moved extensively during our life, we were frequently asked what our favourite place was, a difficult question since each location conjured up its own charm and interest, but if pressed, excepting the climate, Nova Scotia would usually rise to the surface.

The move was almost immediate, and I left Memphis by the end of February 1995. Shelley was left alone with the task of packing up the house, putting it on the market to sell, and liaising with the shipper to take the boat by road to Nova Scotia. The boat left, the house was sold in just one weekend, and Shelley left

Memphis for Sydney, Cape Breton, Nova Scotia at the end of
March 1995.

Our Home in Memphis, Tennessee

Sheraton Casino, Tunica, Mississippi

Shelley at Graceland

Me at Graceland

Chapter Fifteen

The Return to Nova Scotia, Canada

"You may leave Nova Scotia, but you will always return," to paraphrase a traditional Nova Scotian saying. And now we were back, confirming its truth. Back to this beautiful place of hills, valleys and coastlines. People courteous and friendly. Villages traditional and unspoilt, and towns and cities that celebrate summer with joyful festivity and bare winter with good grace and ice hockey.

Back to this place jutting out into the Atlantic Ocean, which, at times, warm and gentle, and times wild, battering the land, the rocky unspoilt coast with wind and wave, always majestic, always beautiful. Back to this place buried deep in our hearts.

After landing in Cape Breton's tiny airport on a connecting flight from Halifax, I took a taxi to the Delta Hotel located in Sydney, on the waterfront, where the management team would reside until they decided to homestead or rent their own accommodations. The company acquired a small building near the casino as pre-opening offices. It contained a reception area and a number of individual rooms where management staff could undertake the tasks required in preparation for August 1, 1995, the casino's scheduled opening date, with construction progressing as planned.

The casino was on George Street, as an addition to the city's Centre 200, an ice hockey arena that could accommodate up to nine thousand patrons for hockey games, concerts, or shows. A section of Centre 200, a large, attached entertainment arcade, had been demolished to make way for the casino, to be built on that site. In March, the various managers were appointed, and they started to arrive in Sydney, experienced casino managers and supervisors from outside Nova Scotia, mostly Canadians from other provinces that already had casinos, and a few from American casinos. Food and beverage, housekeeping, and engineering managers were appointed from within Nova Scotia.

Approximately five hundred employees were required to staff the Sydney Casino, which was a major employment opportunity for this rather depressed area. A three-day job fair was organised in Centre 200 for early May 1995. The fair was designed to interview, hire, and orient a new workforce, and it was a grand event, with entertainment, music, videos about the company, and refreshments provided. All the management staff were on hand to interview and shortlist applicants. Extensive background checks were required, especially for gaming staff, whom the Nova Scotia Gaming Commission would license. This was a lengthy and detailed process, and the RCMP, the 'Canadian Mounties', were involved in checking the backgrounds of applicants nationally, along with coordinating background checks with the FBI on American employees.

The first of my own personal tasks was to view homes for shortlisting, and when Shelley arrived from Memphis, we would choose where to live. Sydney being a small city, this was not a difficult task, and eventually, a nice, detached ranch-style home was purchased on Carmichael Drive, about five kilometres from downtown Sydney and the casino.

It was around this time that we also bought an apartment on a prime, quiet street in downtown Halifax, which we rented out until I would move my office to Halifax the following year. This lovely apartment would remain our home upon my retirement, as we had no plans to ever leave Nova Scotia, which we loved, in spite of the cold winters. In due course, our Toyota, furniture, and boat arrived in Cape Breton. *Sherco*, our sailboat, was redirected to Badeck, where she was offloaded onto Bras D'Or Lakes. *Sherco* had done a 'full circle', and not all on water. She was purchased in Nova Scotia, shipped to St Maarten, sailed from there to Florida, transported by road to Tennessee, and now hauled again by road back to Nova Scotia. As a Bayfield 23, a Canadian boat, she was now home once more.

Following all this activity and a two-month training period, the Sydney Nova Scotia Casino opened its doors permanently on August 1, 1995, operating twenty-four hours a day, 364 days a year. It closed only on Good Friday. It became a popular entertainment destination for locals and visitors alike and enhanced the local economy considerably. Sydney was an industrial town, with the historical economy based largely on mining and steelmaking. That had long ceased to exist, and this new breadwinning opportunity for five hundred families was welcomed by those who needed work and decried by those who needed to invent and sell negative 'fake' news about the casino industry, either in print or otherwise.

Caesars World decided that the two casinos should be named "the Casinos Nova Scotia", like the casino in Tunica, which was named "Sheraton Casino". Caesars was unwilling to dilute the world-recognised iconic name "Caesars Palace". The Halifax Casino had opened a temporary location in the Sheraton Hotel Halifax on June 1, 1995, while awaiting construction of the permanent property, two months prior to the Sydney opening,.

All did not welcome casino gambling coming to Nova Scotia. The senior management teams in both Sydney and Halifax were schooled by the company's public relations consultants on dealing with interviews, questions, and comments by members of the media. I had several interviews, particularly with print media, on human resource issues. Some questions that were posed I answered, and some I had learned to deflect. I was grateful for the guidance from our public relation consultants. There was one thing I learned from this experience, and it was the most blatantly dishonest twisting of what was said, compared with what was printed, all to sell newspapers. I was genuinly shocked to see headlines and articles in several newspapers report comments attributed to me which were absolutely either false, twisted, reversed, or taken out of context. I became a believer that 'fake news' is a reality.

Life took on it's daily routine, the workday week, and on weekends, we would go to Bedeck to sail *Sherco* on the Bras D'or Lake, drive the stunning Cabot Trail around the highlands of northern Cape Breton, visit beaches, or just relax. All these activities were limited to summer and autumn. The kaleidoscope of the colours of autumn in Cape Breton was truly spectacular, with the leaves, from shimmering gold to the deep reds of the maple, intertwined over the hills and down through the valleys.

Winters in Cape Breton were extreme, with mountains of snow and rivers of ice, and behind our house, the forest came right up to our back garden, uninterrupted by fencing. This afforded another dimension of Cape Breton's beauty: the ground wearing a blue-white blanket of snow and the leafless trees covered with coats of sparkling ice, like giant pieces of shimmering jewellery. A winter wonderland!

Two of my greatest challenges in work, which were seriously problematic given their positions, were the people management skills, or rather, lack thereof, of the general manager and the chief engineer. Both were new to the company and came from organisations where management might have been somewhat dictorial. As Sheraton and its subsidiary, Caesars, maintained highly developed employee relations procedures and policies, I needed to coach them on the company's human resource philosophy, a task which led to many discussions, and indeed, not a few arguments.

However, Mel Thomas, senior vice president, who was based in the Halifax Casino but had overall responsibility for the company in Nova Scotia, was very supportive of my efforts. Mel was also new to the company, but he was a knowledgeable manager who made his support for the corporate human resource philosophy very clear. Eventually, the two learned, at least to a tolerable level and this reinforced my continuing strong reputation within the company.

After my father passed away, my mother began to visit family abroad. My father was unwell in later years and was reluctant to travel, so his passing allowed my mother that freedom. She visited my bother, Declan, and his family in Sweden, and in the summer of 1996, she came to see Shelley and I in Cape Breton.

In late 1996, Sherri LeClair was transferred back to a property in the United States. I moved to Halifax, the capital of Nova Scotia, and was promoted to Vice President of Human Resources for the hotel and the two casinos. I now had H.R. responsibility for around two thousand employees, and set about consolidating the three separate human resources departments into one more-effective unit.

I had been in management all my adult life, from the time I was nineteen years of age in Dublin, managing Dartry Dry-cleaning Company, and I was vehemently opposed to trade unionism. While I recognised that in the past, they'd had a purpose during the days of the abusive powers of industrial owners and bosses, I believed that in modern organizations, they were, or should have been, superfluous. I also believed that companies, particularly service organizations, succeeded or failed based on how they treated their employees, who would mirror that treatment with customers. Sheraton's success proved this point. I believed trade unions, especially militant ones, were destructive and existed to support inefficient and disruptive employees from possible termination and, as a business concept, to generate revenue from their fee-paying members.

As the third largest employer in Nova Scotia after the provincial government and the Michelin Tire Manufacturing Plant, Casino Nova Scotia would be a huge prize for the trade unions. I hired the top legal firm in Halifax and worked with their labour lawyers to develop a strategy for the battles I knew would come. And they did! In the years before I retired, there were seven major campaigns by a number of unions attempting to represent the two thousand employees of Casinos Nova Scotia. All failed, and when I retired in 2002, the company remained free of the yolk of trade unionism, with a contented and productive workforce.

The Halifax temporary casino continued operating in the hotel while the permanent one was under construction. The executive offices were temporarily located in an adjoining office tower called Purdy's Wharf, while some offices were squeezed into whatever space was available in the hotel, where every square inch was now a premium.

Scheduled for April 2000, the casino would move to a brand-new, $100 million 'Vegas-style' facility on the downtown Halifax waterfront, and the space the casino occupied in the hotel would be renovated with new bars, restaurants, and function rooms. The new casino would have 650 slot machines and table games. There would be an attached 550-car parkade also under construction. The casino would be connected via pedway to the Sheraton Hotel Halifax. There would be several drinking and dining facilities in the casino, live entertainment at the harbour-front lounge, and concerts, conventions, and other attractions in the Compass Room and the Schooner Room, two showrooms.

The casino has been described as one of the most complicated buildings in the construction company's history. The size of the site meant that part of the building was over water up to seventy feet deep. Most of the land that the casino occupies was created years earlier when that part of Halifax Harbour was in-filled with loose rock and excavation material from other construction sites. The reclaimed land was too soft to serve as a stable building foundation, so the builders overcame the problem by engineering a design which incorporated driving caissons through the fill material and into the bedrock below. Then, using a specially designed doughnut-shaped pile cap as a support system, the engineers worked with the formwork contractor to hang the casino's floor structure on the supporting caissons like a huge wharf. The Halifax Casino was a much larger and more complex construction than the Sydney one, hence the later opening date and larger construction force.

When I moved to Halifax, there were a number of promotions, and one pit manager in Halifax was promoted to shift manager and transferred to the Sydney Casino. Fletcher was a family man, had a house in Bedford just outside of Halifax, and needed a home in Sydney. Fletcher sold his house in Bedford to me, and I sold my house in Sydney to Fletcher, a satisfactory exchange of homes that eliminated a potential problem. The sailboat was shipped by road from Badeck, and I joined the Bedford Yacht Club, where she was moored.

Our daughter Erika, now married to Simon, their one-year-old son, Oliver, their firstborn, two-and-a-half-year-old son, Sebastian—later, as a young adult, he changed his name to Luca— and Simon's two children from a previous marriage visited in the summer of 1998. They thought they might like to move from London to Nova Scotia and sought out opportunities, but eventually, they decided against it. Sometime later, we learned that idea might have been an attempt to save their marriage, which, unknown to us at the time, was in trouble.

Swissair Flight 111 was a scheduled international passenger flight from New York, United States, to Geneva, Switzerland. On September 2, 1998, this flight crashed into the Atlantic Ocean southwest of Halifax Airport. The crash site was a very short eight kilometres offshore from the tiny fishing and tourist village of Peggy's Cove. All 229 passengers and crew aboard died, the second-highest death toll of any air disaster to occur in Canada. The search and rescue response, crash recovery operation, and investigation by the government of Canada took over four years and cost fifty-seven million Canadian dollars.

At ten thirty-one pm on that day, Nova Scotians near the coast felt their homes tremble as the passenger plane smashed into the water. The next morning, when Nova Scotia awoke to the news of this horrific incident, a palpable pall of gloom descended over the whole province, and it remained long thereafter. Just off the beautiful tiny village of Peggy's Cove, which we loved to visit, was now a place of death and destruction.

The flight had taken off from JFK airport and begun to fly over the Atlantic Ocean, but a little less than an hour into the flight, the crew noticed smoke and issued the international urgency signal "pan pan pan." They were cleared to proceed to the airport in Halifax but crashed in the relatively shallow water off Peggy's Cove. The remains of many who were aboard Swissair 111 are buried at a monument near Peggy's Cove. Though only four Canadians were killed on the flight, the crash has had an enduring impact on Canada, and particularly Nova Scotia. Local fishermen led the search for survivors, residents welcomed the victims' families, and the names of the dead are etched in stone monuments at a seaside memorial. Shelley and I had seen and experienced sights of death and destruction in our lives, but this was different. Maybe it was the contrast between the beauty of this place and the ugliness of the incident that made the depression heavier and the gloom darker. It hung not just over Peggy's Cove, but over Halifax, where we lived and worked, like some dark monster. It was a terrible thing! A sad memory even to this day.

On schedule, April 2000, the big move from the Halifax Hotel to the new casino took place. It was a massive operation that took several days to complete. A number of moving companies were hired, and as the casino equipment was being moved out of the hotel, construction companies moved in to start the renovations. Both exercises were carried out with military precision, and the new casino opened its doors on time to great fanfare. The staff, of course, were happy for several reasons. The casino staff would now work in their beautiful new casino, the hotel staff would get their hotel back with a fabulous new renovation, the managers would have uncrowded offices, and the executives could abandon Purdy's tower block and relocate to the executive offices in the casino.

I had a staff of fifteen in the newly consolidated human resources department in Halifax and two in the Sydney Casino, and apart from those in Sydney, we were now all located in our suite of offices on the second floor of the casino. There were four directors reporting to me, one of training and development, one of health and safety, and two of personnel. The various managers covering benefits, organisational design and development, training, safety, and employment, along with their admin staff, reported to these directors. The team was highly motivated and competent, and over the years that followed, they developed several unique human resource systems that substantially contributed to the overall success of the business.

One of my major tasks with Casino Nova Scotia came in 1998, when Hilton mounted a hostile takeover of Sheraton. A 'white knight' was sought, and a small company named Starwood was offered the opportunity to acquire Sheraton and Caesars. Moving the employment relationship of Sheraton/Caesars staff under the Starwood umbrella was a large and complex task that took my full attention into the early part of 1999. Several consultants, along with representatives from both Starwood and Caesars, were involved, with myself as the coordinator and conduit between the parties. A similar process was repeated shortly afterwards, and at the end of 1999, Park Place Entertainment, the gaming division of Hilton Hotels, purchased Caesars World, and I was once more embroiled in the disentanglement of the Nova Scotia components of the companies.

By the time of its completion in mid-2000, I felt I would be soon ready to give it up, throw in the towel, and retire. I felt tired, burned out, and had little left in 'the tank'. My life had been a rollercoaster of successes and failures, all adding to the life experiences I would not have changed, but it had also taken a toll, and though I loved what I did, I felt it soon should end. The year 2002, the sixtieth year of my birth, might be a good time to quit.

In 2001, I advised the company of my decision and met with my staff to make the announcement. One question for them was, who would get the leather chair and the big office? In a subsequent meeting with my two personnel directors, Marilyn Hicks and Christine Tate, to discuss my succession, which would be one of them, Christine voiced her wish not to compete with Marilyn, whom she believed was the best candidate. I agreed, and so the decision was made. The executive committee was informed and accepted my choice. It was announced to all staff that at the end of 2002, Colm Madden would retire. With the takeover by Park Place Entertainment and the winding up of the defined benefit pension plan, I was the last Canadian Sheraton/Caesars employee to receive a pension from the company.

In the seventeen years, from being penniless before going to Bermuda to the time of my retirement, I had been very successful, and while we would not retire rich, we would do so comfortably. We would even survive a substantial hit to our assets in the financial crisis of 2008. Sheraton had been good for me, and me for it. It had been a positive, happy, and productive relationship, and the decision to leave proved a difficult one. It was a decision I felt might have been a mistake, and for several years afterwards, it was one I somewhat regretted.

Around the same time, Erika's marriage was ending, and it seemed divorce was imminent. While Shelley and I had planned to retire in Nova Scotia, we now wished to live nearer to Erika in her time of need, but not in the misery of English or Irish weather, so we decided to sell our apartment in Halifax and our house in Bedford and purchase an apartment in Torrevieja, on the Costa Blanca of Spain, where we planned to live out our retirement. It was nearer to Erika, known to my sister, who had a holiday home there, and warmer than the UK. We sold the furniture, packed our personal effects and our car into a twenty-foot container and shipped it off to Spain, and headed off for a long post-retirement vacation, touring much of India.

While I handed over the HR responsibilities to Marilyn Hicks in December 2002 and left my office and the 'leather chair', I did not officially retire until April of 2003. Rather than take earlier salary increases and bonuses over the previous couple of years, in order to reduce my heavy income tax liability, I converted them into paid vacation and so still had several months on the payroll, although I had terminated my responsibilities.

Halifax Sheraton Casino, Nova Scotia, Canada

Me fourth from the right with the Executive Committee cutting
the ribbon at the opening of the Halifax Casino

The human resources team on retreat in Halifax

Chapter Sixteen

Sailing '*Sixpence*' across the Atlantic

One true story tells of the men and women who risk their lives every working day in fishing boats and rescue vessels, challenging the forces of the sea. Their worst fears materialised on Halloween of 1991, when some of these men and women were confronted by three raging weather fronts which unexpectedly collided off North America in the Atlantic Ocean, to produce the deadliest storm in modern history. Sebastian Junger recounted this event in his book *The Perfect Storm*. Later made into a movie. The tuna fishing vessel the *Andrea Gail* was lost in seas with a recorded maximum wave height of one hundred feet, at that time the highest ever recorded on our planet. The Westsail 32 *Satori*, also caught in this storm, survived it and was later found grounded on a beach intact, a testament to her 'fitness for purpose', although her crew were taken off by a Coast Guard helicopter, which itself was but a hare's breath from disaster.

My goal was to find such a vessel for my trans-Atlantic voyage to Spain and our retirement home in Torrevieja. So, the year before I retired, I sold *Sherco*, our twenty-three-foot Bayfield sailboat, and purchased *Sixpence* a Westsail 32, which I had located in Cape Breton, Nova Scotia. She was a ten-ton displacement, full-keel, canoe-stern, staysail sloop already proven seaworthy during 'the Perfect Storm'. She was not yet in suitable condition to take to the open seas, but she was a fine vessel and would be ready with the time, elbow grease, and money I would lavish upon her.

Sixpence was too large, heavy displaced, and deep-draughted for any mooring in the Bedford Yacht Club, so I joined Armdale Yacht Club, a bigger club with deeper water located at the end of Halifax harbour, nearer the open sea. I was fortunate to obtain a berth, allowing easy access on and off *Sixpence* during the restoration work, avoiding the need to row a loaded dingy back and forth to a mooring.

With the purchase agreed in early summer that same year, I now needed to sail her to Halifax. I enlisted the assistance of Lloyd Melbourne, who was the director of property operations for the Halifax Casino, was a keen sailor, and owned a C&C 29, a popular Canadian-built sailboat. He was happy to undertake the voyage with me from Cape Breton to Halifax, a distance of about two hundred nautical miles. In due course, we drove to Cape Breton and boarded *Sixpence*. I handed over the cheque for C$35,000 and collected the ship's papers, and we set sail for Halifax. We headed toward the short canal at the village of St. Peters leading out of the Bras d'Or Lake and into the open Atlantic, rounding the head at Canso, bound for Liscomb, where we planned to spend the first night.

On the second day, we headed for Sheet Harbour, to overnight for the final time before making for Halifax and *Sixpence's* new berth. As yet unfamiliar with the boat and, indeed, this North-East coastline of Nova Scotia, we chose to avoid night sailing, though both of us had sailed previously on the South coast of the province. The weather was fine but cool, with a moderate wind that filled her sails as *Sixpence* scudded along at a steady five to six knots. The voyage was enjoyable and uneventful, and I was delighted with the performance of my new vessel. Arriving at Armdale Yacht Club late Sunday evening, just as the sun was setting in an orange-tinted sky, we tied up *Sixpence* alongside her berth, and headed home for hot showers, hot food, and cold beers. I slept well that night, confident that I had the right boat to face the Atlantic Ocean.

Over the two summers that followed, Shelley and I enjoyed sailing and entertaining friends on *Sixpence* around Halifax Harbour, Bedford Basin, and Nova Scotia South Shore. With a full keel and heavy displacement, she was not easy to sail in relatively tight spaces, and tacking was a challenge. Getting her to 'come about' in light breezes in the harbour or in the basin required more speed than she could sometimes muster. Being caught 'in irons' necessitated pulling and pushing of boom and sails, and a quick spurt of the engine was a frequent occurrence. But of course, this was not her purpose, and in due time, she was to become much happier on the open ocean.

Whenever we were not sailing, I spent hundreds of hours on her renovation and tens of thousands of dollars on her re-equipment, both before and after my retirement. *Sixpence* had a substantial quantity of wood and wood finish, and while the hull and deck were fibreglass and gelcoat construction in excellent condition, all interior bulkheads, cabinetry, cabin sole, seating, berths, and headliner beams, along with the external cap-rail, bowsprit, bow platform, and hatches, were solid wood or lined with wood, and all with varnish that was badly peeled, scratched, or faded. I spent the first whole winter of weekends stripping and re-varnishing all this wood.

There was a heater onboard, so inside work was undertaken without discomfort. Canadian winters, however, are not conducive to working outside, so the bowsprit, platform, and hatches were dismantled from the boat and brought to the casino engineering department, where they were restored with the help and expertise of the chief engineer, Sandy Urquart, supported by the ample supply of tools that would make for a more efficient workload.

In the spring of 2002, before the sailing season began, the woodwork restoration was completed and looking beautiful. New upholstery was in place, and several pieces of new 'kit' were on order. I was awaiting delivery of an offshore four-man canister life raft that would be mounted on the boat's deck, a Jordan Series Drogue to slow our run in the event we encountered a serious storm, a Cape Horn wind vane self-steering system, and an EPIRB. A new set of Doyle sails was being built in Halifax, and the sailmaker would also install new standing and running rigging. Other new equipment included two GPS devices, two self-tailing genoa winches, batteries, solar panels, battery-charging systems, and a whole bunch of other bits and bobs, all of this to make for a safer, more secure, and enjoyable voyage.

Following our post-retirement tour of India, I returned to Canada in April 2003 to continue preparing *Sixpence* to face the Atlantic Ocean, while Shelley remained in Calcutta to spend more time with her siblings. Joe McGuinness, the food and beverage director for the casino and hotel, offered to accommodate me in his home for the couple of months I was back in Halifax.

The goal was to sail out of Halifax Harbour in early June of that year so *Sixpence* would be well out to sea before the start of the hurricane season. There were still several tasks awaiting completion, not the least of which was to find crew. Four would allow for safer watch rotation, with two on deck at all times, particularly important during the blackness of the night or in heavy weather. During the previous summer of 2002, Henrik Brameus, who was a Swedish friend of Nazli Shapanto, Shelley's niece who lived in the Netherlands, had expressed an interest in the voyage. He'd flown to Nova Scotia to meet me and sail with me for a week. Joined by Shelley, the three of us sailed *Sixpence* back up to Cape Breton, around Bras d'Or Lake, and then back to Halifax, a round trip of over four hundred nautical miles. The chemistry worked; Henrik loved how *Sixpence* sailed, and he signed on as crew, confirming he would return in 2003 for the trans-Atlantic voyage.

With Henrik and myself, the crew was now two. I would ideally have liked to have two more, but was prepared to leave with three people if I could find one more volunteer. I placed an advertisement for two volunteer crew on the notice boards of the yacht clubs and boatyards around Halifax, Dartmouth, and Bedford. I soon had interest from Mannie Laufer, a very knowledgeable and experienced sailor who had his own boat, which he sailed on regular occasions from Nova Scotia to Bermuda, and wanted to do a trans-Atlantic crossing. He also taught navigation at some of the local colleges, so I was very happy to have him as the third member of the crew.

Todd Armstrong was a young man from the Canadian Prairies. He had never been on a sailboat and had only viewed the ocean for the first time when he came to Nova Scotia. He was hoping to find an inexpensive way to get to Europe, his big adventure. Seeing my ad. on the notice board of Armdale Yacht Club, he approached me to offer his services. I was absolutely adamant I would not take him on, for I believed Todd would be more of a hindrance than a help. Furthermore, I didn't want the responsibility if we were caught in heavy weather or a storm. I would rather sail with just myself, Mannie, and Henrik.

I was now ready to haul *Sixpence* out of the water to complete the work still required. I resigned from Armdale Yacht Club, sailed around to Dartmouth boatyard in Bedford basin, and had her lifted out of the water onto 'the hard'. It was April 2003, and over the next two months, I would complete the engineering work. The propeller was removed, and then the drive shaft. A new cutlass bearing, stuffing box, drive shaft, water, and fuel tanks were installed. Chainplates and through hull fittings were checked and replaced where necessary.

During this time, Todd Andrews was a frequent visitor to the boatyard. He continually requested he be considered as crew, and with no other volunteer forthcoming, I finally succumbed to his pleadings. Todd assured me that he would be useful, as he was a professional cook and would willingly do all the cooking. As it transpired, he was absolutely brilliant at converting canned and dry food into gourmet meals, and we were well fed throughout the voyage. However Todd's lack of exposure to the sea and sailing limited his ability to perform other tasks, and much of his time during the voyage was spent horizontally in his bunk or, when on watch, horizontally on the deck.

In early June of 2003, *Sixpence* was finally ready and was launched back into Bedford Basin. The mast was stepped with new rigging and new sails. The penultimate task before provisioning was to swing the compass, which we did, with deviations noted. Henrik arrived from the Netherlands and moved on board. Mannie lived in Halifax, and he would board on the day of departure, with myself doing likewise.

We did have a fifth crew member, but he would not be sailing and had never even seen *Sixpence*. Jiri Soukup lived in Toronto and was a friend of Mannie's and would monitor the weather on the internet. We agreed on a fixed UTC (Coordinated Universal Time) to call him daily on the satellite phone, when he would provide a forecast for the lat/long position where we were. This would greatly assist in course changes should heavy weather be headed our way.

Sixpence was provisioned and then sailed from Dartmouth Boatyard over to Purdy's Wharf in Halifax to await the day of departure. I visited the harbour master to register my sail plan, providing details of *Sixpence*, our voyage, radio call sign, satellite phone number, expected latitudes and longitudes, and our arrival dates in the Azores, Gibraltar, and final destination, Torrevieja Spain.

I bid my farewell to Shelley, expecting, hoping, to see her on the other side of the 'pond', and on June 11, 2003, with instruments and watches set to UTC, we slipped shorelines and, at UTC 13.50, eased the bow off Purdy's Wharf, and on that warm, bright, sunny day, we motored out of Halifax Harbour.   I called Halifax

Harbour Radio on the VHF to advise them of our departure. By UTC 15.15, we passed south of McNabs Island on the outer edge of Halifax Harbour. The wind picked up sufficiently to hoist the sails, one reef in the main, staysail full, and genoa fifty percent, and the engine was switched off.

Sixpence soon settled into her stride, revelling in her relationship with wind and wave, happy she was no longer constrained to twist and turn on tacks in confined spaces but allowed to run free, straight out onto the open ocean like a turtle anxiously leaving the beach for the sea. She picked up speed to 5.2 knots, then 5.4, and soon 6.0. A rhumb line course was set southeast to the first waypoint, the self steering wind vane was deployed, and the crew settled down to a hot coffee, secure in the belief *Sixpence* was happy, willing, and able to keep us safe.

At UTC 00.10 on June 12, the barometer started to drop. It was cold and damp, and the wind was blowing at fifteen knots, but *Sixpence* was happy, and so were we. Two on deck on the first four-hour watch, warmly wrapped up against cold and wind, and two in the bunks. By UTC 15.15, twenty fours after departure, the log showed 135 nautical miles had been covered through the water and 172 nautical miles over ground, a stunning pace helped by tides and currents. Some have suggested the Westsail 32 is slow, lumbering, and overbuilt. *Sixpence* would prove them very wrong and would continue to do so throughout the voyage, hitting nine to ten knots at times.

The barometer was still falling, and we were now in the Labrador Current, in thick fog, and the wind had dropped. The direction from where sound comes in fog at sea is extremely difficult to judge, but we blew the foghorn at regular intervals. With visibility of only a few meters, the sailing was nerve-wracking.

The fog cleared, the wind rose, we were sailing up to 6.6 knots, and *Sixpence* was happy once more. But suddenly, off the port bow, a large container ship appeared within approximately two kilometres. Travelling at about twenty knots, it was much too close for comfort. My quickly repeated calls on VHF Channel 16 fell on deaf ears; no response was received. With a quick change of course, engine on, revs up, a potentially disastrous situation was just narrowly averted. It was shocking irresponsibility of the container ship's crew failing to monitor their radio.

UTC 04.00 on June 13, the wind had veered north and dropped. We furled the sails and started the engine. By UTC 19.00 that same day, fifteen hours later, the wind rose, and we hoisted sail and shut off the engine. By UTC21.20 on June 14, we completed the rhumb line course, arriving at waypoint lat. 40.10 N and long. 57.24 W. We reset the wind vane and changed to an easterly direction on a great circle course headed directly for the Azores.

We were now almost five hundred nautical miles from Halifax, and the wind was now from the south at twenty-two knots, gusting up to twenty-six. The weather was warming, all sails were full, and *Sixpence* was charging along at 6.5 to 7.0 knots. For three days, we sailed under beautiful conditions, with pods of dolphins racing the boat off the bow. At night, the brilliance of a non-light-polluted sky exhibited the magnificence of a billion twinkling stars, and their radiance seemed reflected in the blue-green luminescence of the plankton in *Sixpence's* wake, nature's jewellery, which shone and shimmered like sapphires floating on the ocean's surface. This was a truly magical place, where the essence of nature, untouched by human hand, was a spiritual experience. But this was the Atlantic Ocean, and Jiri advised us by satellite phone that we should soon prepare for the onslaught of some heavy weather.

By UTC 12.50, June 15, the wind had veered west, blowing steadily at twenty-five knots. The sea had begun to rise and was now at two metres. The wind continued to increase, and the seas continued to rise. By 16.45, the wind was a steady forty knots, gusting to forty five, and the seas were confused and now at six to seven metres. As the black and angry waves broke, white spume blew off their tops.

I decided to deploy the Jordon Series Drogue. We attached the bridle to the stern and let it run out, all 250 metres, with a cone parachute every metre and a heavy chain at its tail to keep it taut. We secured the tiller amidships, checked to make sure the appropriate navigation lights were on, and battened down the hatches to await the storm's passing. *Sixpence* settled into a rhythm, rising and falling with the waves and her shrouds whistling with the wind. I did not permit alcohol to be consumed during the trip, but Mannie brought along a bottle of high-quality tequila he was saving for our arrival in the Azores. Since Jiri's forecast indicated it could be forty-eight hours before the passing of the storm, and as it was now June 16, my birthday, all agreed the bottle should be opened while we awaited improvement in the weather. We were relaxed and confident from how well *Sixpence* was riding wind and wave—well, maybe Todd was not quite so relaxed.

Sixty-five hours after we deployed the drogue, the storm passed, the wind died and at UTC 10.00 on June the 18th we hauled in the drogue and started the engine. I had a small pulsing wristband, not unlike a watch, which I wore to ward off seasickness, and it worked exceptionally well. Mannie and Henrik were somewhat affected by the sea state during the storm, but Todd was a concern. He was quite unwell, and I remembered my friend Cyril from years earlier, when we'd sailed from Southampton to Northern Ireland. Cyril had been so seasick he'd hardly been able to move from his bunk. We were now six hundred miles offshore, so no help could be forthcoming, but Todd braved it out and fought through the illness. He was young, fit, and healthy, useful under the circumstances.

Two strange occurrences puzzled me following the storm. I began to mildly hallucinate. First, when off watch at night in my bunk, I would hear voices in conversation. While I was unable to decipher the languages spoken or the topics discussed, I knew for certain they were human voices. These were not dreams, for I was wide awake and only heard them at night and not when off watch in my bunk during daylight hours. The second phenomenon occurred while on watch on deck, just at the point dusk was turning to darkness. I would see on the horizon, city skylines with modern skyscrapers of varying height, just the outline, no details. Of course, we were in the middle of the Atlantic Ocean, and it was an impossible though unnerving experience, one without explanation.

The ocean is a strange place for a small boat. It seems not that great expanse of water seen from an airplane or from atop a hill overlooking the sea, and instead is but a tiny self-contained body of water, carrying its vessel along, alone in the universe. With *Sixpence's* deck less than three feet from sea level and her crew about six feet above that, due to the curvature of the earth, the horizon was but about four nautical miles in all directions, and for the sailors on a small boat in the midst of this great ocean, that's all there is, their small moving body of water, beyond which there is nothing, a void. It is the place where one truly lives in the moment.

At UTC 15.30 that same day, the wind picked up from the southwest at sixteen knots. We hoisted sail and shut off the engine. Barometric pressure was 1025 and rising. For the next two days, there was lovely weather and steady sailing. Todd continued to provide tasty meals and then immediately return to his bunk, or when on watch, he did so horizontally in the cockpit.

On the morning of June 20, the wind dropped, but the engine failed to start. I climbed into the engine compartment to check and discovered that the transmission fluid had leaked and the transmission was seized. We now could only hope for continually favourable winds until we reached Horta Harbour in the Azores, still about eight days away. By UTC 17.00, the wind had picked up to twenty-five knots, and we changed course to the south to avoid a low pressure system Jiri had reported on the satellite phone. We opened the staysail fully, the genoa to seventy-five percent, and the main with one reef. *Sixpence* reared up and took off: 6.0 knots, 6.3, 6.8, 7.0, 7.3, 7.5, she was sailing effortlessly and would achieve her fastest twenty-four-hour run for the whole voyage, covering 160 nautical miles at an average 6.66 knots.

June 21, at UTC19.20, we had to tack hard to avoid a container ship. Once more, there was no response to my calls on Channel 16, a repeat of our earlier experience. These kinds of incidents I later lerned, are unfortunately not entirely uncommon on the high seas. While we were four and therefore always with two of us on watch, the danger to single hand sailors while they sleep, is a greater risk.

As hoped for, we sailed steadily and without incident for the next five days, and on June 28, at UTC, we sighted Horta. With no engine power, we were faced with the tricky task of sailing *Sixpence* right up to the dock to berth her. This is an easy manoeuvre with a small sailing dinghy, but it's quite a different matter with a ten-ton offshore sailboat in a tiny and unknown harbour. Very careful planning was required. What direction and speed was the wind in the harbour? How much space was there to tack? Were there any other boats leaving or arriving? Where would we come alongside? Those and a myriad of other questions were considered.

As it was Henrik's watch on the tiller, he would take *Sixpence* in. I was on the bow, with bowline and Mannie on the stern. Todd would be amidships, ready to fend off. We would wait until we were inside the harbour to decide whether to dock port or starboard to the pier. With some very tight tacking and no small amount of nail-biting, Henrik pulled off a masterful stroke of helming, and we tied up *Sixpence* at the arrival pier in Horta on the island of Faial in the Azores at UTC 11.15 on June 28, 2003, seventeen days from Halifax, Nova Scotia, and within two hours of my original estimated time of arrival.

I brought the passports and the ship's papers to the customs and immigration office and received clearance, and the four of us headed to the nearest pub for cold beers and hot steaks. Then Henrik set about continuing a tradition of the Azores, painting our story on the pier. This tradition has existed as a measure of good luck for those on the perilous voyage across the ocean, and a number of the multitude of paintings decorating the pier date back many years. Pots of paint of a variety of colours were left for any new arrivals, and Henrik painted a picture of *Sixpence* with the crew's four names at each corner and the name of our destination at the bottom.

Horta was a stopping point for sailboats crossing the Atlantic, mainly those sailing east from North America. Boats sailing west from Europe tended to cross further south. About three hundred boats per year stopped in Horta, so there were a well-stocked chandler and a good selection of eating and drinking places, of which Peter's Pub was the one most frequented by the sailing fraternity. Faial Island is located about five miles across a channel from Pico, which has the highest point in all of Portugal's territories, including the homeland itself. Faial is approximately sixty-seven square miles in area, with fifteen thousand inhabitants. Horta is the capital, and blue is their colour. Different shades of blue decorate the houses, divide the fields, and line the roadsides; hence the island is oft referred to as "the Blue Island". In 1957, a volcanic eruption occurred which propelled large quantities of lava and ash onto the landscape. The crew of *Sixpence* took time out to visit this ash desert set amongst the green of the rest of the Island.

The following day, Todd, Mannie, and Henrik took a ferry over to spend time on Pico while I remained in Horta to oversee repairs to *Sixpence*. The transmission was indeed seized, and I sent to the UK for a replacement to be flown out as quickly as possible. This took several days and a substantial chunk of cash, a necessary though unwelcome expenditure. Once repairs were completed, following an eight-day break in Faial, on July 6 at UTC 09.00, we slipped the shore lines and motored out of Horta Harbour. It was a beautiful, warm day, and by UTC 12.00, under a clear blue sky and a steady breeze of twelve knots, we hoisted full sail and set the wind vane on a course for the Strait of Gibraltar.

On the four days that followed, the wind blew steadily around fourteen to sixteen knots. The sails were full, the sun shone in a cloudless sky during the day and a billion stars twinkled at night, the dolphins continued to race *Sixpence*, and the cook kept us well fed, having restocked in Horta. During the afternoon of July 12, while I was alone on deck, a massive whale breached about one hundred meters off the port bow. Unfortunately, it happened both too suddenly and unexpectedly to catch on camera. No other witness to this extraordinary sight.

By the night of July 14, we were sailing in moderate breezes and kindly seas in the separation zone of the shipping lanes off the southern coast of Spain. In the blackness of night, we could see the lights of dozens of ships moving with us off the starboard side and in the opposite direction off the port side. It was an awesome sight, and though we were a minuscule dot on the ocean in comparison, we relished the sense of companionship. We were no longer alone, constrained by the limited horizons of our tiny lake in motion.

On July 15, at UTC 22.30, we arrived at Trafalgar light and passed into the Strait of Gibraltar, arriving off Gibraltar on July 16 at UTC 08.00. It was an arduous struggle through the strait as *Sixpence* fought an outgoing tide of about four knots as the Mediterranean poured into the Atlantic. With the engine running, the speed through the water at about six knots moved us over ground at only two. It seemed at times that we were stationary. However, we had successfully crossed the Atlantic Ocean, and I had fulfilled a lifelong sailing dream. We had planned to spend a few days in Gibraltar, climb the big rock to see the local monkeys and enjoy some good food and cold beers. Unfortunatly it was not to be. We heard on the radio that a serious viral epedemic was rampant there and Gibraltar best avoided. Now all that was left was a day and a half through the Mediterranean to Torrevieja, *Sixpence's* new home port.

Mother Nature, however, had not yet finished with us. By UTC 20.00 on July 16, the wind had risen to twenty-eight knots with following seas which broke over the stern on more than a few occasions, flooding the cockpit. We fitted the washboard in the cabin hatch furled the mainsail and continued to sail downwind on partial headsails alone, toward our final destination.

July 17, UTC 08.00, the wind was gentle, the pink skyed dawn was breaking, and the crew of *Sixpence* washed, shaved, and changed into fresh shorts and t-shirts. By 10.00 hours, off the port bow, the skyline of Torrevieja came into view. I radioed Club Nautico to advise of our imminent arrival. I had, before departing Canada, contacted them for a berth. *Sixpence* would be berthed Mediterranean style, bow to the dock, anchor off the stern.

At UTC 12.00 that same day, *Sixpence* slipped into her new berth, the stern actor was dropped, the bowline was made fast, and her crew came ashore to be greeted by Shelley, Erika, Luca, Olly, and some friends. Champagne corks were popped, and balloons and streamers were let loose. We had sailed 'through the water' a distance of 3,174 nautical miles in a total time of thirty-five days, twenty-two hours, and ten minutes. A voyage completed!

Following a couple of days at our new apartment in Aldea del Mar, the crew departed. Mannie returned to Canada, Henrik went back to Sweden, and Todd left on his great adventure, touring around Europe. And Shelley and I were left to our retirement.

June 11, 2003, *Sixpence* is ready for the Atlantic crossing

Friend Eric (not sailing) and I June 11, 2003, the day of departure

Chapter Seventeen
Retirement, the Final Chapter

December 15, 2002, was My final workday with ITT Sheraton, Sheraton Hotels Corp., Caesars World, Park Place Entertainment, and Casino Nova Scotia. It was under the same organisational umbrella I had worked for over the past fifteen years, although the company's history of mergers, acquisitions, realignments, and name changes might suggest otherwise. On the eve of retirement day, the company held a cocktail party to honour me and bid me farewell. It was formatted in the style of *This Is Your Life*, a popular TV program from earlier years which outlined the careers of chosen celebrities.

It was a lavish affair attended by current staff, a number of colleagues from my previous time in Halifax, who were now in senior positions in other hotels throughout the city, and the labour lawyers I had worked closely with while battling trade unions. As an acknowledgement of the respect and affection for me, the human resources staff jointly composed and read out the following poem.

Ode to Colm Madden

There was an HR VP
Who came from across the wide sea
From the Emerald Isle,
And he stayed quite a while.
He's quite a guy, don't you agree?

His dad worked for labour, you see
Was as pro-union as one could be,
Colm told us one night,
And if he is right,
That apple fell far from THAT tree.

Colm's done a lot since he's been here
Like drinking red wine and dark beer
But surely, we kid.
There's more stuff he did.
We'll speak of them all while we're here.

He's held lots of jobs, it is true.
In Sydney and St Maarten too.
From his spot on the beach,
All employees, he'd teach.
What a tough job, yeah, boo-hoo for you.

The man could be calm as a lamb.
He could also be kind of a ham.
When he got upset,
It would be a sure bet
We'd grab our day-timers and scram.

Just one other thing we did dread.

When we saw Colm rubbing his head,
We knew he was stressed
Or timing was pressed.
It meant "Don't talk; just listen instead."

But let's put all kidding aside.
There's one thing HR must confide.
We want him to know
Even though he must go
We think of him with love and with pride.

So we've all gathered here on this day,
For soon he'll be sailing away.
He's leaving for Spain,
And though our hearts are in pain,
We wish him blue skies all the way.

Many messages of congratulations were received from colleagues and friends around the world, a number of which contained amusing anecdotes of times we spent together.

The party ended, and retirement began!

On December 18, 2002, Shelley and I departed beautiful Nova Scotia and flew to Dublin, Ireland. We celebrated Christmas in Bray, Co Wicklow, with Erika, Luca, and Olly. Following her divorce Erika had moved to Ireland. In late January 2003 Shelley and I left for Kolkata (Calcutta) and our post-retirement two-month tour of India. We had fulfilled that Nova Scotian proverb, again paraphrased: "If you leave, you will always return to Nova Scotia," and we did, and it would not be the last time. While we would never again live there, we would always carry that special place deep in our hearts, and unable to resist a 'sentimental journey', we returned to Nova Scotia on vacation in 2010.

Arriving in Kolkata, we stayed with Shelley's family for a few days to recover from the long journey. On the appointed day, the first of our post-retirement tour, we took a taxi from Boral where the Roy Paladhy home was, to Howrah Station for the train journey to Delhi. We planned to stay with Shelley's nephew Sudeep, his wife, Shyamalee, and their young daughter, Maya, in their home in Gurgaon, on the outskirts of Delhi. That would be our base from which to visit various historical locations in North India. We subsequently expanded the tour to include much of South India, and on Sudeep's recommendation, also spent a week in Goa, a popular holiday destination on the West Coast of the country.

The train, which was scheduled to depart at ten a.m., was delayed, and eventually, we left at ten pm, twelve hours late. This, just to confirm we were now in India. While a two-hour flight would have been more efficient, we wanted to enjoy views of the countryside and towns along the way, hence, the decision to travel by train. Unfortunately, throughout the forty-hour journey, nothing was visible as dense fog blanketed field, forest, and hamlet—a disappointing start to our Indian adventure. Sudeep, unaware of the train delay, generously and tirelessly waited hour after hour at the main station in Delhi for our arrival.

We spent an exciting two weeks in North India, visiting many places of historical significance in Delhi. Humayun's Tomb, the Red Fort, and Qutub Minar to name a few. We took a train to Agra and a taxi to see Fatehpuri Sikri, the capital of the Mogul Empire, and then it was on to Agra Fort and, finally, the Taj Mahal. Many have seen pictures of the Taj Mahal, but to be physically in its presence is to view something breathtaking. It is truly stunning, perfectly proportionally constructed from shimmering white marble, originally embedded with precious stones which, of course, are no longer there. Unfortunately, the surging economic growth of India, with its industrialisation and ever-increasing pollution, is impacting negatively on this precious world heritage monument. We also travelled to the Hawa Mahal, or the Pink

Palace, in Jaipur and to several forts throughout Rajasthan.

With Sudeep driving, he, Shyamalee, Maya, Shelley, and I spent our penultimate weekend in Northern India at the Mud Fort in Kuchesar. This is now a hotel and part of the Neemrana Hotel chain, which specialises in converting palaces and forts from the long-past days of the kings and maharajas, into luxury hotels. One magnificent example of these properties was the Neemrana Fort Palace in Rajasthan, where Shelley and I spent our final weekend in Northern India, a stunning restored regal edifice from that golden era.

Then we flew to Goa for a relaxing week to enjoy the expansive beaches with their shacks serving fresh seafood and cold drinks, and the tropical vista of swaying palm trees and emerald green paddy fields. We stayed in the Cavala Inn, a small hotel with a well-patronised, lively bar owned by Sudeep's friend Marius. Goa impressed us and I wondered what it might be like to live there. India's smallest state, Goa was formerly a Portuguese colony that gained its independence and was co-opted into the Indian Federation in 1961. It still maintained somewhat of a Portuguese flavour with an Indian twist.

The week ended, and we flew from Goa to Cochin in Kerala. Keralites proudly refer to their state as "God's country", and with every justification. It is truly spectacular and recognised as such, not only by the sons and daughters of the soil, but by many Indians at large. From the tea gardens of Munnar atop high mountains boasting the highest tea garden in the world, to the backwaters of its lowlands, where Shelley and I spent time on a houseboat slowly meandering through the rivers and canals that crossed bright green paddy fields, small wooded areas, and tiny villages, to the 'Chinese' fishermen in Cochin City, we experienced a week of wonder in "God's country".

From Cochin we journeyed by train to Kanyakumari, at the southern tip of India in Tamil Nadu. There we watched the lamplights of the fishing boats coming ashore at dawn, the crowds on the beach facing east to welcome the rising sun as it ascended over the Bay of Bengal. That same evening, we strolled along the water's edge of the Indian Ocean and watched the sun setting over the Arabian Sea. We took a boat ride over to the two islands—well, large rocks, in reality—where the Vivekananda Mandayam and the enormous forty-metre statue of Thiruvalluvar are located. We spent two days in Kanyakumari, rented a car, and continued our tour through the temple cities of Tamil Nadu, Thanjavur, Madhuri, Tiruchy, and Kanchipuram, a week of soaking up the magnificence of the temples and the stories of their history.

Next stop was Pondichery, the ex-colony of France. It still maintains a French Quarter, very French, where the police wear uniforms with the round pillbox caps. The road signs were in French, with French names, and the restaurants served excellent French food from French menus. A few hours of absolute peace and reflection at Aurobindo Ashram and a visit to Auroville were just some of the other highlights of the Pondichery stop. After two days, it was back on the road for the two-hour drive to Chennai and a flight to Kolkata. We had come full circle.

It was now mid-March, and having completed our holiday tour of India, I left for Torrevieja on the Costa Blanca of Spain and our new home in Aldea del Mar. Shelley remained until the end of March, spending additional time with her siblings in Calcutta (Kolkata).

Earlier that year, Erika had decided that she wished to live closer to her parents. It was a difficult time for her after her divorce, so she sold her house in Bray, moved to Spain with her two children, and stayed in our apartment while searching for a place of her own. She eventually purchased a home, also in Aldea del Mar.

On March 31, I received the sad news from Dublin that my mother had passed away. Unfortunately, Shelley learned of this while en route from Calcutta, and she arrived in Torrevieja the day after Betty died. She and I flew from Spain to Dublin on April 2, 2003, for the funeral. We returned to Torrevieja together, and on April 22, I left for Halifax, Nova Scotia, to complete preparations for the trans-Atlantic crossing.

Aldea del Mar is a beautiful complex that won several architectural awards. It is but a couple of hundred meters from the nearest beach and consists of seven buildings, approximately three hundred apartments with dozens of varying designs, layouts, and sizes. The buildings surround lush gardens and a large, freeform swimming pool. We planned this to be final retirement home.

Our retirement dream was to sail *Sixpence*, around the Mediterranean, beginning with day sails, then progressing to weekends, and eventually for longer periods and farther shores. This proved a pipe dream. While in Canada, Bermuda, and Ireland, during the summer months, dozens of white sails were visible, carrying their sailboats along the coast, either cruising or racing. But off the Costa Blanca shore, we saw the very rare flutter of sails in the breeze. The yacht harbours were full of boats, but it seemed they sailed nowhere. Active sailors like myself would refer to them, somewhat disparagingly, as "gin palaces". The coast had little or no natural coves or harbours where a small boat could drop anchor, so the only option would be to berth in a commercial yacht harbour, of which there were several. But no berths for visiting yachts were usually available as they were all occupied by the 'gin palaces'.

Sixpence never left her berth at the Club Nautico Torrevieja and a final impediment to sailing her occurred in the winter of 2004 when a freak squall charged through Torrevieja's narrow harbour entrance, pushing the surging sea before her. It lifted *Sixpence* out of the water and smashed her bow against the club's stone wharf. Thousands of euros in damages were incurred, and the boat was craned out of the water for repairs, which took six months to complete.

I sold her, for one is lost who loses confidence in their ship. *Sixpence* had safely carried my three companions and I more than three thousand nautical miles, through two storms across the Atlantic Ocean and the Mediterranean Sea, yet it was in the 'safety' of a harbour that she almost met her demise.

I felt it was important to immerse myself in the community of Aldea del Mar, and when invited, I joined the residents' management committee. I was elected chairman, and while I willingly took on the role, it proved to be more of a challenge than expected.

With a mixture of residents from a variety of nationalities and socio-economic backgrounds, from millionaires to simpler folk, from Spanish to foreigners, and from newcomers to long-term residents, each had different priorities. In my attempt to address all their concerns, I found the role untenable. At the end of my term, December 2004, at the Annual General Meeting, a new committee was elected with a Spanish chairman; this was, in fact, more appropriate.

As time passed, Erika's boys needed their father more frequently than he could visit Spain, and she decided to sell her apartment and return to England. Her apartment sold quickly, and I handled the proceeds of the sale on her behalf. The process was indeed strange: part of the funds were in cash, usually about forty percent, and the remaining sixty percent was paid by cheque or bank draft. In Erika's case, it was twenty percent in cash, forty thousand euros. Although this was actually illegal, it was a practice countenanced by all. This included the lawyers and notaries for both parties, who would leave their office while the cash was being transferred from the purchaser to the vendor, so as not to be party to an illegal act. This custom was tantamount to being mandatory whether one wanted to participate or not.

At the conclusion of the transaction, I left the lawyer's office in downtown Torrevieja with a cheque and forty thousand euros in cash stuffed in every pocket. In preparation, I'd worn a multi-pocketed jacket and cargo shorts. I drove straight to the bank to deposit the funds in Erika's account. As this was a regular ocurrence, bank employees were completely aware of how to deal with the situation. The manager of the bank where Erika, Shelley and I each had accounts advised me that I should deposit less than six thousand euros at a time; otherwise, I would draw the attention of the tax authorities. I should also leave several days between deposits. So, fifty-nine hundred euros immediately went into Erika's account, a further five thousand went into Erika's account identified as the sale of furniture, not taxable, fifty-nine hundred went into my account, fifty-nine hundred went into Shelley's account, and the balance of the cash was stuffed into the wall safe in our apartment. It took two more weeks to deposit the rest, with the funds subsequently transferred to Erika's U.K. bank.

While Aldea del Mar was beautiful, outside its gates Torrevieja was a concrete jungle. High-rise apartment buildings crowded the narrow streets, which were devoid of a blade of grass, a tree, or a shrub. The city had a permanent population of approximately one hundred thousand, which, in the summer months, swelled to six hundred thousand. Every square inch of the tiny beaches was occupied by sunbathing bodies, elbow to elbow. As the summer residents departed at the end of August, the apartment buildings were shut and shuttered, restaurants closed, and the town seemed as if deserted. Our apartment complex soon began to fill me with a sense of claustrophobia, like a luxury prison. Drive in through the gates, and it's an oasis of green and of calm; drive out, and you're in the jungle, the concrete jungle! I began to reminisce on the beautiful, expansive beaches and the lush green growth of Goa.

A couple moved into the apartment above us, an Englishman and a Scandinavian woman, and very soon, they became a blight on our tranquillity. 'Neighbours from Hell'! Constant drunken fights, arguments, shouts and screams were accompanied by the spewing of foul language occurring at all times of the day and late into the night. And this behaviour continued even at children playing below. This went on day after day, night after night, and no amount of communication from me changed this behaviour.

By the end of 2005, we thought that maybe a move might be prudent. Remembering Goa, in January 2006 we went back there for two months to see if this was the place we should relocate to. Sudeep, Shelley's nephew, had a friend, Margaret, who lived in the village of Tivim in the district of Bardez in Goa. She was a writer like Sudeep and owned a house in the village of Aldona, which was rented to a young couple. The couple was leaving Goa for a two-month extended vacation, so the timing was perfect, and Margaret and her tenants agreed to sublet the house, including their two dogs, to us.

So began our day-to-day 'Living in Goa Project'. We had two months to experience Goa, tour the towns and villages of India's smallest state, absorb a sense of the culture and cultural activities, and research the availability of basic needs, food, shelter, general cost of living, and, most importantly, of homes should we decide that Goa was for us. Margaret had a motor scooter, which she lent us, so we had transport, which we used extensively to tour the narrow roads and lanes of Goa..

We viewed many homes, but nothing appealed to us and time was passing quickly. Near the end of our stay, we were shown one final property, an old 'Goan Portuguese' house in Aldona—well, ruin would more aptly describe it. It was built in 1872 and had last been occupied in 1984. The site was over four thousand square metres, but the house and the land were completely overgrown. The place was a jungle, the roof had long since collapsed, and a tree was growing out from where the dining room used to be. But it had potential and was on a prime site in a premier village.

The real estate agent introduced us to a builder, one Charles

Pais, who assured us he could renovate the property. Others were more sceptical, not necessarily about the ability of the builder, but more about the ability of the ruin to withstand renovation. We now had to make a decision on two major steps: would we purchase this ruin, and would we move to Goa? Following much deliberation, and with some trepidation and even a slight degree of desperation, we decided to do both. I paid a deposit on the 'ruin' and agreed to hire the builder to renovate it. I believed it was important to maintain the original layout as much as possible, and I designed how I wanted the house to look when completed. I presented a concept drawing to the builder, who agreed that he could accomplish the task and had his architect finalise the required architectural drawings.

The decision to relocate to Goa made, home found, and deposit paid, we returned to Torrevieja to put our apartment on the market. It sold quickly, and in August 2006, we departed Spain for Goa, with Shelley determinedly stating that this would be the final time she was prepared to move regardless of what the future might hold. For forty years, she had travelled with me from place to place, country to country, continent to continent in support of me, without objection or complaint, so back in her homeland, I knew she had a right to that position.

We rented a house in Corona, a ward of the village of Aldona and close to where we'd stayed earlier in January. It was a couple of kilometres from the new home in Ranoi, another part of the village. This would allow me the opportunity to keep close contact with the builder and review progress on the renovation.

The renovation was to take eight months, but it took two years of arguments, disagreements, misunderstandings, and misinterpretations. At one point, the builder physically threatened me. It was a difficult two years, and while we made friends and enjoyed life in Goa, the concern for how the house was progressing was a source of constant stress. Many times, there was no one on the site, and when challenged about that and the slow progress, the builder would often become abusive. The construction contract called for staged payments, and as several payments were already made, some in advance of their schedule in order to facilitate the construction, I was inextricably tied to Mr Pais. The relationship deteriorated to the extent that Charles Pais eventually walked off the job with the house incomplete. And ten years later, a legal suit filed by me against Charles Pais is still proceeding in the court in Goa.

We moved into the unfinished house in August of 2006. Over the next two years, we completed the internal jobs that remained, the construction of the swimming pool and pool deck area, the construction of the boundary wall, garage, and parking area, and the landscaping of the grounds. Our home rose like a Phoenix from the ashes, from a ruin to a house admired by friends and neighbours for its welcoming feeling, its tastefulness, and for what had been accomplished.

In January of 2009, my two sisters and their husbands travelled from Ireland to Goa to spend five weeks with us, and we toured South India. Following a week of relaxation in Goa, the three couples began three weeks 'on the road', returning to the places Shelley and I first visited in 2003.

Shelley and I settled into the routine of normal life in our beautiful home in Aldona over the next eight years. Shelley visited her family in Kolkata yearly. I would accompany her every few years, and both of us would go to the UK for a couple of months each year during India's monsoon season. I purchased a thirty-six-foot Catamaran in England on which we planned to live aboard and sail during our annual UK visits. However, there were several problems related to *Safari Blue*, as the boat was named, and I subsequently sold her and purchased a holiday home instead. My sailing life had come to an end. Erika and her two children came to Goa every Christmas during their school holidays.

One could spend a lifetime visiting places of interest both natural and of historical significance in India, yet there would always be more to experience.

Our next big trip was to Sikkim, nestled in the Himalayan Mountains. In January of 2010, Shelley and I flew to Kolkata, travelled by overnight train to Siliguri, and from there, rented a car and drove through Northern West Bengal up into the Himalayan Mountains to the state of Sikkim, towards its capital, Gangtok. The entire state is hilly, and Kanchenjunga, the world's third-highest peak at 8,586 metres, situated on the border between Sikkim and Nepal, was visible with its shimmering white blanket of snow as our car slowly climbed its way higher and higher. While about a third of the state is forested, the land is largely unfit for agriculture because of the rocky, precipitous slopes, although we did notice some hillsides had been cut into and converted into small terraced farms. The Himalayan Mountains surround Sikkim on three sides, and several mountain passes connect Sikkim to Tibet, Bhutan, and Nepal.

We eventually arrived at our hotel in Gangtok, a small city on the side of the mountains with a fascinating array of shops selling all types of local craft items along small streets too narrow for traffic and restricted to pedestrians. While there, we visited the world-famous Rumtek Monastery, revered among Buddhists, especially Tibetan Buddhists, which includes a beautiful shrine temple and a monastery for the monks. The original monastery was built in the sixteenth century, and the new one was completed in 1966.

The following morning, we continued our climb into North Sikkim, into the Himalaya foothills. For this, we had organised a large four-wheel-drive SUV, a driver, a guide, and a supply of food to bring to Lachung, the last town before the Tibetan border just fifty kilometres distance. The Indian army has control over a large portion of the northern part of the state, as Sikkim forms part of a sensitive border area with China. Since many areas were restricted, we required official permits to visit them. As we journeyed, the mountains grew taller, the snow deeper, and the cliffs along the precarious road steeper. We arrived safely at our destination by late afternoon.

The town is at an elevation of about 9,600 feet, and at that time of the year, January, it was bitterly cold, covered in snow, and dark. We were the only two guests of the small, rather primitive hotel, hence the need to bring our own supply of food. our room was basic, with two tiny single beds and an old-fashioned electric fire with one rather weak heating bar. By about five pm, the village was in darkness, and we learned that in winter, people went to bed around that time as there was little else to do in the cold with limited heating options available. We did likewise.

We spent two weeks touring Sikkim, enjoying many historical sites among the majestic mountains, valleys, rivers, and lakes of this beautiful state. Rejuvenated and inspired by our time there, we returned to Goa and to our home routine.

The following year, we went to the Sunderbans on the delta of the mighty Ganges River. We rented a tour boat and, over a three-day weekend, traversed the waterways of the Ganges Delta, hoping to see a Bengal tiger, but unfortunately, that was not to be.

In 2015, I was diagnosed with colon cancer and underwent successful surgery. However, our beautiful house, acre of gardens, and swimming pool with extensive deck area became too much to manage inspite of having a full time gardner and housekeeper, so we sold the house the following year and purchased an apartment. In March of 2017, I was again the subject of a medical drama when I was rushed to hospital with a subdural hematoma. Following two major brain surgeries over three days, I quickly recovered due to the work of superb surgeons, my own positive attitude, and the prayers and good vibes of family and friends, and I returned home to our new apartment in Salvador do Mundo, Goa, where we continue to live.

Shelley enjoys retirement in Goa

Our home in Aldona, Goa

Shelley, my sisters and I in Kerala

Me in Munnar, Kerala

Epilogue

In my twilight years, as I look back over my career, I feel enormously grateful for the joy and satisfaction my work life has provided and know that both the lows as well as the highs contributed value to my life's experiences. While I recognised that my decision to resign from InterContinental Hotels early in my career, probably deprived me of a steady climb through the ranks to a senior corporate position, it might very well have proven just a little too predictable.

While this is my story, and since 1966, when we met those many decades ago, it is of course also my wife's. Shelley has been my rock through the ups and downs of our life together. She may view our life through a different prism, but she would be the one to recount her own tale.

This is but part of the story, for there are roads I've been down, rivers I've sat beside, hills I've rambled over, valleys I've walked through, experiences I've felt and people I've met whose names and places are unremembered, but their pictures are saved in the albums of my memory. There are many who, through my mentorship, have climbed their own ladder of success, and for that, which I believe, after my family, was my life's purpose and for which I am most proud.

It is now 2020. Shelley and I have lived in Goa for almost fourteen years, far longer than we have lived anywhere else in our more than half a century of married life, and we will most likely spend our final days here. Do I belong here? Maybe, maybe not, but I am here, and where else could I be? Goa is now my home. I do not belong to the country of my birth, Ireland. I feel like a stranger there. I do not belong to the country of my heart, Canada, for I abandoned her. I oft feel like a fragile tree, like the papaya tree that sprouted from seed to maturity in our garden in Aldona, the village where we lived when we first settled in Goa. It gave of its fruits but eventually collapsed, for it was not completely rooted to the ground upon which it stood. Like that papaya tree, I, too, am not completely rooted to the ground upon which I stand, for my roots are nowhere or everywhere, weakened by their constant shifting. This is the price I paid for the life I've lived, for the privilege of being to the places I have been, for knowing the people I have met, for working with them, living with them, and being a guest in their countries. I willingly paid that price, for the journey through my work life has been a joyful and satisfying one that I am grateful for and would not have changed. While the highs have been breathtakingly beyond my expectations, and the lows difficult and sometimes dangerous, all are part of the tapestry of life and are interwoven through the experiences that have enhanced my journey more than I could ever have dreamed.

I do have but one regret: the burden upon my daughter, Erika, that this journey has bestowed. Ten schools in twelve years made a fully rounded education untenable, and this was unfair to her, denying her a place in which to feel a permanency, to have lifelong friends, with memories of growing up with those friends. There are occasions, however, when I sense she may be ambivalent about this. During the good times, Erika lived a comfortable and experiential childhood, often in far-flung, exotic places, in a variety of different locations. And even in the difficult times, she suffered little deprivation. She now lives in Folkestone, Kent, in the United Kingdom with her two adult children, Luca and Oliver. Unsurprisingly, given her childhood experiences, she claims now to live in her "never again moving" home.

I live a quiet life with Shelley in Goa, where we leave for several months every monsoon season to spend time with our daughter and grandchildren in Kent. We have a holiday home there and relish our independence, along with the opportunity to spend time with our small family. We enjoy Goa, the green of the tropical vegetation, the blue of the cloudless sky before and after the monsoon, the warmth of the sun, the sandy, expansive beaches, the beach shacks where fresh seafood and cold beer is readily available, and the friendship of all those we have come to know. With this, Shelley is at peace, as am I—for the most part! But my peace is schizophrenic, for I am intolerant and impatient, burdened by my unrealistic expectations of others. It frustrates my personal capacity for task and challenge; thus, I have little patience for the converse, of which much exists here.

In Goa, I continue to battle against my dark side. I chase my demons, unable to put them to the sword. They surfaced infrequently during my work life but are a constant in my retirement. Perhaps work was my solace! I have learned to consider, at least, that much of the characteristics portrayed in astrological symbolism may have some merit in fact, for I could truly be considered a classic Gemini, and hard as I try in the twilight of my years to unify them, those characteristics remain juxtaposed. So far, I have failed to escape my other darker self, but that battle continues.

The papaya tree at Aldona House, Goa